LOVE IS PRAXIS

Lydia Ocasio-Stoutenburg and
Yuchen Yang (eds.)

LOVE IS PRAXIS

Lived Experience-to-Classroom Lessons Through the Voices of Disabled Students, Practitioners, Mothers, and Siblings

The Disability Studies Collection

Collection Editors

Damian Mellifont &
Jennifer Smith-Merry

First published in 2024 by Lived Places Publishing

All rights reserved. No part of this publication may be reproduced, stored in a retrieval system, or transmitted in any form or by any means, electronic, mechanical, photocopying, recording or otherwise, without prior permission in writing from the publisher.

No part of this book may be used or reproduced in any manner for the purpose of training artificial intelligence technologies or systems. In accordance with Article 4(3) of the Digital Single Market Directive 2019/790, Lived Places Publishing expressly reserves this work from the text and data mining exception.

The authors and editors have made every effort to ensure the accuracy of information contained in this publication, but assume no responsibility for any errors, inaccuracies, inconsistencies and omissions. Likewise, every effort has been made to contact copyright holders. If any copyright material has been reproduced unwittingly and without permission the Publisher will gladly receive information enabling them to rectify any error or omission in subsequent editions.

Copyright © 2024 Lived Places Publishing

British Library Cataloguing in Publication Data
A CIP record for this book is available from the British Library

ISBN: 9781916985063 (pbk)
ISBN: 9781916985070 (ePDF)
ISBN: 9781916985087 (ePUB)

The right of Lydia Ocasio-Stoutenburg and Yuchen Yang to be identified as the Volume Editors of this work has been asserted by them in accordance with the Copyright, Design and Patents Act 1988.

Cover design by Fiachra McCarthy
Book design by Rachel Trolove of Twin Trail Design
Typeset by Newgen Publishing UK

Lived Places Publishing
Long Island
New York 11789

www.livedplacespublishing.com

I dedicate this chapter to the students and individuals who find reflections of their own experiences within my story. In moments when support seems rare and mentors are inaccessible, always remember that you are your own greatest source of inspiration. Above all, my heartfelt dedication goes to my parents, who fought for our family, and to my sister, who would fight to whatever end.

—Aimee

To my chosen family, the Kosko-Blyler family, my college professors, and all the other individuals who have touched my life. I wouldn't have gotten this far without you all.

—Ava

To every learner who has ever experienced being an outsider in a place that ought to feel like home—I dedicate this chapter to you. May our schools one day become a site of safety.

—Azaria

To my brother. My life revolves around you, and my heart will always be yours.

—Bianca

I dedicate this chapter to anyone who resonates with my story. Know you are not alone, and your courage is remarkable. And to my family, especially my sister. You are the reason for everything I am and everything I will become. Kerri, you are my "why" forever and always.

—Courtney

This chapter is dedicated to all of the beautiful and courageous children and their families who welcomed me as a member of their support teams. I will forever cherish all of the ups and downs we worked through together.

—Dana

This chapter is dedicated to my younger self. To the person who went through countless years of pain and to the person who thought she was the problem. My experiences have inspired me to fight harder to be better. This is also a reflection of things I went through and gratitude for those in my life.

—Jenna

To my family. I could not have done this without you, and this is all for you.

—Julia

This is for all those who have guided me with their remarkable strength. Particularly, to the exceptional individuals with disabilities that I have had the privilege to cross paths with; thank you for imparting meaningful insights on empathy, insightfulness, and boundless capabilities present in each one of us.

—Karla

I dedicate this book to my family. And to the authors of the chapters in this book and their families, whose stories, courage, resilience, tears, and dreams fill the pages of this book. I am grateful for each and every one of you.

—Lydia

To Sage, thank you for always choosing one more day. To CEM, SGM, and NLM. You make me a better person, and I'm so proud to be your Mamí. To my mom and dad cheering me on in heaven, I love you and miss you so much. To everyone who has supported me and helped me learn and grow…Thank you.

—Millie

To all the women with disabilities who never stop fighting for their rights.

—Nayma

To my big brother, Ian Zinn, who inspires me and challenges me to be a better and more compassionate person every day.

—Rebecca

To the amazing young man who made me a mama, and the eight beautiful loves who came after. To my beloved abuelita Lola who showed me the meaning of true love.

—Ruby

To those who give voice to the voiceless and strength to the struggle, the special education professionals and family advocates, this dedication is for you. Your compassion and dedication light the way for others.

—Yuchen

Abstract

Disabled people, their caregivers, and family members are often on the receiving end of decisions by service providers and professionals. Family members are often positioned as inexpert in relationships with school professionals, which often carries over into how disabled students are perceived, as well as the opportunities provided for them. These experiences are not uncommon, and can transcend from early intervention to the higher educational context. This book captures the stories of students with disabilities, siblings, practitioners, and caregivers who describe their own ways of knowing, theorizing, identity affirmations, and life navigation, within the school context. Drawing from bell hooks' framing of love as praxis, the authors challenge us to reimagine the classroom as a transformative space. In doing so, we can reposition people across disability, racialized and social identity, familial, cultural, and multiply marginalized lived experiences as experts in their own lives.

Keywords

caregivers, culture, disability, education, family, intersectionality, lived experience, love, practitioner, students

Contents

Foreword: What's Love Got to Do with It?   xi
Beth Harry

A Note on Language   xvi

Content Warning   xvii

Introduction   xviii

Learning Objectives   xxiii

Chapter 1   A Parent's Fight: Nurturing Identity, Overcoming Adversity   1
Aimee Granada-Jeronimo

Chapter 2   Older-Younger Sister: The Unknown Middle Child   9
Rebecca Zinn

Chapter 3   Mama Bear   29
Millie Rodríguez

Chapter 4   It's Complicated   49
Dana Patenaude

Chapter 5   Too Much…Not Enough   69
Julia Sledz

Chapter 6   Speaking Out: A Letter to the Reader   73
Karla Patricia Armendariz

x   Love is Praxis

Chapter 7	"Listen" *Bianca Emma Stoutenburg*	**89**
Chapter 8	How Does It Feel to Be a Woman with a Disability in a Developing Country? *Nayma Sultana Mim*	**99**
Chapter 9	Finding Myself through Autism *Ava Herr*	**111**
Chapter 10	School as a Site of Resistance: Becoming an Advocate *Azaria Cunningham*	**135**
Chapter 11	Empowering Exceptionality: A Mother's Call for Collaborative Understanding in Education *Ruby Humphris*	**145**
Chapter 12	Kerri's Way: Family, Lessons, and Memoir *Courtney Kehoe*	**155**
Chapter 13	The System Failed Me, but I Did Not Personally Fail *Jenna Spencer*	**165**
Notes		**192**
References		**194**
Notes on Contributors		**199**
Index		**205**

Foreword

What's Love Got to Do with It?

The narratives in this book argue that love has everything to do with education. But where would we go for guidance on how to infuse love into a special education system driven by legalistic and bureaucratic structures? In the introduction to the book, the author states that our educational system has traditionally been framed as "passionless and objective, without care". While many may disagree, claiming that school personnel do care about their students, I believe that thoughtful reflection on the way education professionals are trained does support this view. My guess is that a qualitative analysis of the goals of most teacher preparation manuals, and even research reports in leading professional journals of education, would reveal a great deal more about strategies, goals, assessment, and lesson planning than about caring, feeling, or bonding between teachers and their students.

Moreover, I think it is true to say that professional training typically advises budding teachers and therapists not to become "too involved" with their students. The purpose of this approach is to be able to maintain an objective understanding of students' strengths and limitations. By this view, the setting of personal boundaries is an essential part of professional work, establishing what we believe is a clear line between objective and subjective knowledge. The latter is generally assumed to be less reliable and

xii Love is Praxis

less valid. This principle may well hold in relation to the generalized knowledge gleaned from studies of large groups, but it can only be a starting point when working with an individual. At the individual level, we are faced with a whole person whose lived experience presents us with endless contradictions and conundrums that may defy our professional preparation. Listening and watching with love provides the way through this.

This is not to say that we can ignore the difference between a professional and a personal relationship. How do we achieve the needed balance? This book utilizes a range of lenses for viewing this challenge. Through the eyes of siblings, parents, teachers, paraprofessionals, and self-advocates, we become immersed in the highly nuanced and unpredictable ways in which our work can be informed and, indeed, transformed by love.

For example, in Chapter 4, "It's Complicated", the author offers a detailed chronology of her experience of "highs and lows" with a family with whom she formed a strong relationship over several years, but which ultimately ended when it became evident that the services she and her colleagues could offer were no longer adequate for the child and family. The narrative hints at the challenge of becoming so committed to a child and family that the inevitable leaving of that relationship becomes problematic. The delicate balance needed here quivers in the background of this narrative, yet the author concludes that the rewards of work that is informed by love make it all worthwhile.

In Chapter 7, "Listen", a sibling of a boy with Down Syndrome describes how the power of love provides a kind of in-depth, totally subjectively acquired knowledge of the needs of a child who is nonspeaking:

> We use the alternative and augmentative (AAC) device to help him express his needs and wants, but a part of me hoped that he wouldn't have to talk through a tablet. So much can be lost through translation, such as if he so happened to change his mind in a split second on whether he wants cookies and cream ice cream or an ice cream sandwich. And I wouldn't know, because I was too busy looking into the freezer to notice that his facial expressions have changed, and he's signaling me to pay attention to him.

But the lens provided by siblings is by no means monolithic. The author quoted above teaches us about the power of a sibling's bond to read the unspoken communications of a loved one, while also straddling the intersections of her brother's disability and Black identity. Here, the author reflects on how the intersection of racism and ableism often intensifies the social negativity of which her brother, in his innocence, is unaware. The author of Chapter 2, "Older-Younger Sister: The Unknown Middle Child", reveals yet another dilemma as she struggles to find a balance between being the younger and yet the more competent sibling. She details her efforts to develop the self-conscious learning needed to find her footing in a family structure that defies stereotypical expectations and roles.

The lenses of mothers provide us with numerous lessons on the power of parental advocacy. We become aware of how easily professionals can slip into a "we-they" relationship with parents, closing ranks with colleagues in order to protect our professional status. Instead, we need to ask ourselves the following questions: In excluding or dismissing parents' views, is it my goal to enhance the student's development, or is it a self-defensive reflex intended to fend off demands that I fear might tax my energy or test the boundaries I've established between myself and those advocating for something new for a child? Are my decisions driven by bureaucratic guidelines by which the checking of a required box allows me to believe my job is complete? Or are they guided by responsiveness to information being provided by someone who loves and knows the child way more than I ever will?

With regard to the importance of love in learning from individuals with disabilities themselves, a key issue is the self-image being developed by the individual. These narratives point to the tension between one's intuitive knowledge of oneself and the internalizing of the negative views others hold of us. We see the importance of external supports that nurture self-confidence and a positive self-image. Children learn not only by cookie-cutter positive reinforcers, but by a touch, a look, or a hug that conveys love and approval to a child who might be receiving rejection and humiliation from a cruel and uncaring world.

So, back to my opening question: Where would we go for guidance? I suggest that we turn to the dynamic process of Cultural Reciprocity developed by Kalyanpur and Harry (2012), which calls for us to learn from others whose familial and cultural practices differ from professional expectations. In this approach, we begin by developing within ourselves a sharp awareness of any biases and assumptions that may hinder our ability to listen to and respect views and experiences that differ from ours. Putting our biases on hold, we can listen to the voices of those who know and love the child, respectfully acknowledging their perspectives. We then reciprocate by sharing our professional understandings and goals, so that both sets of perspectives are respected and taken into account in a process of collaborative decision-making. Thus, love and professional knowledge go hand in hand, thus creating a praxis tailored to the context of an individual's real and daily life.

My last word to teachers in training would be: Do not be afraid to learn from love and to love your students. Your professional training will be enhanced and will still be there to help you keep your balance.

Beth Harry, PhD

Professor Emerita

University of Miami

A Note on Language

This book contains terminology that may not be universally sound, with meaning that is bound to the historical, legal, or contemporary context. In addition, some of the terminology may be archaic and/or offensive to some communities that are shifting away from the negative and deficit-based connotations of the terms. One example is special education, which in the US represents a set of services and supports that serve disabled children there, while also encompassing a set of protective laws. Many disability rights groups and organizations are moving away from the word "special" which has often been used to discriminate against disabled people. Another such term is "disabled"—while in some contexts, person-first language is preferred, in others, identity-first language, such as "autistic person", is preferred. With that said, we make no claim that language is neutral, for it is situated and constructed around norms that change over time and context. Instead, we note that each of the authors has questioned, troubled, decided upon, or resisted many of the terms, some of which may be placed in quotations to illustrate how the author pushes back on the term.

Content Warning

This book contains explicit references to, and descriptions of, situations that may cause distress. This includes references to and descriptions of the following:

- Suicidal thoughts, intentions, and actions
- Eating disorder behaviors
- Psychiatric inpatient centers and experiences
- Graphic descriptions of acute physical or psychological health crises
- Grief and loss
- Trauma
- Violent assault, sexual violence, and bullying
- Ableism, racism, discrimination, and microaggressions
- Applied Behavioral Analysis (ABA) (although the term in particular, and the field in general, is not universally a cause of distress, some people may have had harmful experiences where any mention of these may cause distressing memories to resurface).

Introduction

When bell hooks spoke about love, it was as if it were the most radical notion. Love, through its energy, power, and insistence, is rarely perceived as a praxis, that is, the theoretical and abstract put into practice. In dicussions about teaching, hooks centered love, a positioning that runs countercultural to the framing of most of our educational system, which is often viewed as passionless and objective, and without care. Instead, hooks (1994) redefined love as a "core foundation" and one that "humanizes" (p. 131). The classroom is not a place devoid of emotion or even conflict, for that matter, as hooks described the importance of weaving in elements of care even for moving through points of pain. Hooks added so powerfully, "we bring to the classroom settings our unresolved fears and anxieties...the loving classroom is one in which students are taught both by the presence and practice of the teacher, that critical exchange that can take place without diminishing anyone's spirit, that conflict that can be resolved constructively" (p. 135).

We think about "conflict" as it has occurred throughout our lives, in our classrooms, in our communities, and through the injustices we feel for people who are most marginalized in the school systems. The conflict is historical, where people with disabilities, their caregivers, People of Color with disabilities, and people experiencing multiple marginalizations have been harmed. Schools have also been complicit in that harm. Disabled people, their caregivers, and even their providers are often positioned as inexpert receivers of information instead of being perceived as constructors of knowledge who bring rich perspectives into the classroom context.

Through personal narratives and critical ethnography, this book is a portraiture of disability and love through the lived experiences of disabled young adults, practitioners, emerging professionals, and family members. Drawing from bell hooks' centering of love as transformative praxis, it includes testimonies of people whose lived experience repositions them as knowledge-bearers, even when their ways of knowing, learning, practicing, and valuing have been discounted by those around them. Each story introduces their lives in time and context, valuing them as educators who teach others, both informally and formally. This book is a harmony of generational, familial, collegial, and cultural expressions of love.

You'll notice that there is an interwoven structure of the book, from the personal disability narrative to the practitioner lens, from the sibling's devotion to a mother's love. This tapestry of stories provides a rich and deep introspection that underscores how important it is to value all forms of wisdom. Embedded in the chapter texts are elements of storytelling, global perspectives, poetic cadences, and freewriting. The authors are pre-service educators, emerging research scholars, practitioners, and some who share more than one of these identities. There are stories of pain, memory, hope, frustration, and calls for justice. Undeniably, at the center, is love.

Chapter 1, "A Parent's Fight: Nurturing Identity, Overcoming Adversity", describes Aimee Granada-Jeronimo's experiences

xx   Love is Praxis

growing up in an environment where teachers failed to support and understand her disability. Despite how disability, cultural, and familial biases manifested in difficult school experiences for her, she pursues her goal of becoming a supportive special education classroom teacher. Chapter 2, "Older-Younger Sister: The Unknown Middle Child", with its story and meaningful title crafted by Rebecca Zinn, discusses the ways in which the author challenges community (mis)perceptions of disability while navigating the world with her brother who has autism.

We move out to the family level in "Mama Bear", Chapter 3, in which Millie Rodríguez details her battle as a mother of a twice-exceptional child, fighting for her child to be supported in K-12 and transitioning into the higher education context. Emphasizing the need for caring and empathetic practitioners, Dana Patenaude highlights the interdependent and complex relationship with families in Chapter 4 titled "It's Complicated". We revisit the personal disability narrative in Julia Sledz's "Too Much…Not Enough", Chapter 5, which outlines practitioners' dismissals of the lived experience of disabled people, emphasizing how even with the complexity of issues, a transformed system is needed, where the status quo is never enough. In Chapter 6, "Speaking Out: A Letter to the Reader", Karla Patricia Armendariz describes the importance of child and family voice that acknowledges systemic issues from the practitioner's view while advocating for change. In "Listen", Chapter 7, Bianca Emma Stoutenburg traces her painful, real, and loving journey as a sister of someone with a disability. She describes the tensions of her prayers for her brother while recognizing the need to advocate for him, which involves a simple choice that prioritizes listening and love.

Chapter 8, "How Does It Feel to Be a Woman with a Disability in a Developing Country?" by Nayma Sultana Mim, provides a rich, intersectional, global perspective that builds upon the theme of practitioner reflection, while also advocating for future policy directions. Ava Herr's "Finding Myself through Autism", Chapter 9, draws the reader back into the closer, more intimate point of view with the personal experience of disability, sibling bonding, and personal growth as a future special educator. In Chapter 10, "School as a Site of Resistance: Becoming an Advocate", a former schoolteacher and emerging education scholar Azaria Cunningham builds upon the theme of pre-service teachers acknowledging the system level and interpersonal biases in education. She achieves this by raising her voice and using poetry to describe/impact a flawed system through advocacy.

Revisiting a mother's perspective in Chapter 11, Ruby Humphris' "Empowering Exceptionality: A Mother's Call for Collaborative Understanding in Education" describes her own journey from her son's diagnosis to advocating for appropriate school support, while also challenging professionals to shift from their deficit views through advocacy. "Kerri's Way: Family, Lessons, and Memoir" by Courtney Kehoe (Chapter 12) takes the reader back to the sibling perspective. Filled with emotions and professional aspirations, the chapter conveys hope. Finally, we round out our chapters with a powerful story by Jenna Spencer in Chapter 13 titled "The System Failed Me, but I Did Not Personally Fail". This chapter echoes the presence of systemic failures found in the prior testimonials, describing how pervasive it is across systems. Jenna's story highlights a journey of

xxii Love is Praxis

self-advocacy, resilience, personal growth, and empowerment through narrative storytelling.

With each author providing reflection questions for the reader, this book is for emerging teachers as well as those providing both general education and special education services. The book is also for other education personnel, which include not only paraprofessionals, staff, and administrators but also those responsible for generating curriculum. As our work centers on disability in school, this book is also essential for related service professionals who, by lending their hands, provide much-needed support and services to students to celebrate every goal. Also aimed at faculty who prepare the next generations of classroom teachers to expand their ways of knowing, as well as people who are conducting research on the impact of incorporating diverse and multiple perspectives, this work contextualizes and broadens their understanding of lived experience.

We hope the reader will appreciate the richness, power, reality, and upliftment conveyed through these stories of unbridled love.

Lydia Ocasio-Stoutenburg and Yuchen Yang, Editors

Learning Objectives

In this book, the reader will learn about the following:

1. The multiple, contextual, cultural, and complex perspectives on the experience of disability.
2. The role that practitioners, family members, peers, and all members of the community play in the individual's experiences, as well as that of their caregivers and siblings.
3. The challenges in the systems and support that exist for people with disabilities and the ways in which they need to change.
4. How people who lead with an ethic of love care for, believe in, and advocate for people with disabilities, and how this informs their future practice.

1
A Parent's Fight: Nurturing Identity, Overcoming Adversity

Aimee Granada-Jeronimo

I was only five years old when my kindergarten teacher slapped me across the face. The moment her hand touched my face, I felt the air escape my lungs. I was incredibly confused as I did not understand why my teacher had just hit me. My twin sister sat in front of me, equally confused and hopeless, unsure of what to do. It took all of my energy to try not to cry and show my teacher how much she had hurt me at that moment. I did not know how to react or what to do as I was always taught by my parents to respect my teachers and elders, and so I remained silent. This was one of the first moments I remember remaining silent when I should have spoken up for myself instead, and it certainly was not the last time. It was only until my sister worked up the courage to tell my parents what had happened that we found out the reason that my teacher slapped me.

My sister was and will forever be my biggest supporter, right alongside my parents. My parents escaped poverty and war and came to America to find a better life for themselves—the iconic "American Dream". They never expected to find each other—two people of Portuguese heritage—in America and to fall in love and create a family. From the day they had my sister and me, they were committed to making sure that we had the life they could have only ever dreamed of having as children. Newark, New Jersey, was my parents' home for 13 years. It was a place where they could freely express their culture, language, and love for each other as two women without fear, but they knew it was not the place where they wanted to raise children. They saved up all their money and moved to our forever home in Caldwell, New Jersey, where I was born and raised.

Sadly, when my parents moved to Caldwell, they faced a new type of war—a war of hatred and discrimination. As immigrants, English language learners, and gay women, the intersectionality of their identities caused them to face discrimination on a daily basis in the heteronormative and homogeneous town. The thing that my parents feared most was that my sister and I would also face the effects of hate because of who they are. To try and minimize that amount of discrimination we would face on a daily basis, and because my parents could not afford childcare in Caldwell, my sister and I went to preschool in the Ironbound of Newark, my parents' safe haven and the one place that my parents felt comfortable being their true authentic selves.

Newark is a city of diversity, a place where the difference in the human population is celebrated rather than feared. It is where my family was welcomed with open arms; it was our home. My preschool welcomed my sister and me without hesitation, two twin girls who were only three years old and spoke no English, as they accepted children from all backgrounds—children whose stories were similar to mine. Our teachers embraced students of all races, ethnicities, and cultures and taught their students to do the same. My teachers never saw my background as a hindrance to my education but instead understood the importance of my diversity and how it would help shape me into the person I am today.

I faced a big culture shock when I started kindergarten in Caldwell, a place where my house was, but not my home. It was confusing to be learning in an environment in which I was forced to speak only English, in a place where students all shared the same background, and where cultural diversity was lacking, as I had never learned in an environment like it before. My parents always greatly valued education, as it was something that they did not have the joy of easily receiving growing up. They understood that we were lucky enough to live in Caldwell, a place in which we could receive a good, free, public education. They never expected that my sister and I would face as many barriers as we did when they made the decision for us to attend school in the town in which we lived.

The slap across my face was the first of the many challenges that I would face in my education and life. As soon as my parents came to know of the situation, they contacted the school

4   Love is Praxis

to find out what had happened. The school was "not aware" of the situation but agreed to facilitate a meeting with my parents and the teacher. When questioned about the situation, the teacher admitted to slapping me but deemed it an acceptable reaction because she did not like how slowly I was turning the pages of my math workbook, and she wanted me to find the page faster. My parents were extremely upset over the situation, but they felt like they had no power or voice to make a change, and thus, without facing any repercussions, she continued to be my teacher. However, my parents were assured that nothing like this would happen again.

Little did I know at the time, and little did my teacher know, that I have a learning disability[1] and auditory processing disorder[2]. This affects my auditory understanding and makes verbal directions hard for me to follow. I was not just turning the page of my book slowly; I had not understood which page to turn to as the classroom was noisy, as most kindergarten classes are, and I was trying to figure out what to do by looking at the page my peers were on. This was one of the first times my disabilities impacted me, but it would not be the last, and it took more than three years for me to even be diagnosed with a learning disability.

After many similar instances with other teachers and with my grades being poor, especially in language arts, my parents began to relentlessly push for me to be evaluated for a learning disability. However, my school was reluctant to have me tested. Looking back, I wonder whether the intersectionality of my parents' identities made it convenient for my school to overlook their concerns because how could two women—two immigrant women with accents—discover my challenges before the professionals at my school could?

My difficulties were always attributed to the fact that English was not my first language, despite the fact that I was fluent in English by the age of four. Several researchers have described this misperception that teachers have about students (e.g. Hamayan et al., 2023). My school as well as the teachers used this one fact against my parents' concerns and encouraged them to speak to me only in English, as they felt that my difficulties would quickly pass once English was the only language I was using to learn and communicate. This was not true because they failed to recognize that I was having the same difficulties with my first language, Portuguese, which is an indication that I could have a learning disability.

My school overlooked a crucial understanding: that parents, caregivers, and families of children with disabilities possess unparalleled insight and knowledge about their child's difficulties and needs, second only to the individuals with the disabilities themselves. My parents understood me better than I understood myself at the time, and they knew that the challenges I was facing did not just have to do with the fact that English was not my first language. Hence, they continued to fight for me and for the education that I deserved. This involved going to many doctors and psychologists to get answers. I, along with my parents, never realized how a disability label would impact my life along with all my other identities. After receiving my diagnosis, I was no longer just the daughter of gay immigrants but the "disabled" daughter of two gay immigrants, and this additional label haunted me for many years.

The hate and hardships I faced in relation to my disability naturally made me shy away from my disability identity. I did not want to be known as a student who received accommodations and is a part of the disability community because of my negative experiences. Now, I have grown to love every part of who I am and can recognize that my disability is what makes me uniquely me and should be highlighted and not dismissed. I realized that I could use my newfound love for my disability to empower others. In the end, I did not let my new label of having a disability stop me from doing what I wanted to do most in life.

Despite many obstacles, I have had a passion for teaching since I was a child. The challenges I encountered with my teachers fueled my determination to ensure that my future students would not have to endure the same hardships. Had I not faced such adversities throughout my educational career, I would not be the person, and a future teacher, that I am today. I never understood my full purpose in life until I got older and realized the power and knowledge I hold as a person with a disability teaching students with disabilities. My unique background of having a disability and receiving special education services makes me uniquely qualified to teach students with disabilities, as it makes me a more kind, caring, and compassionate teacher because I can wholeheartedly relate to and understand the emotions that my students are feeling and the challenges they may face.

Since I can remember, disability has shaped every aspect of my life and will continue to do so for the rest of my life. So instead of hiding away from it and not acknowledging it, I celebrate it every day, recognizing that it helped shape me into the person and future teacher I will become. Had it not been for my kindergarten teacher, who slapped an innocent, shy, and nervous little girl, I would not have transformed into the confident and strong-willed woman that I am today. I will fight for students and people with disabilities across the world every day, the same way that my parents continually fought for their little girl.

Reflective questions

1. Reflect on the importance of cultural competence in special education settings. How do you make sure you are creating a supportive and inclusive learning environment for students with disabilities, especially those from diverse cultural and linguistic backgrounds?

2. In what ways can educators empower students with disabilities to embrace their identities and be self-advocates, especially in environments where discrimination may exist?

3. Consider the role of parental love and support in identifying and addressing the needs of students with disabilities. How can educators effectively collaborate with parents to support their child's educational journey through a foundation of love and understanding?

2
Older-Younger Sister: The Unknown Middle Child

Rebecca Zinn

At just three years old, I could already tell that my five-year-old brother wasn't like me. Not because he's older or because he's a boy and I'm a girl, but rather I was starting to notice that I couldn't even hold a conversation with him. That same year my mom explained to me that my big brother, Ian, had autism. His autism was making him do and understand things differently than most people. Now I knew that **he** was different, but I quickly realized that my whole family was being treated differently too. No one else's family got the piercing stares we did while walking through the Payless shoe store. No one else's older brother was as loud as mine or flapped his arms when he got excited, causing others to look, ask that he quiet down, or even ask that my family leave.

At first, the dynamic between my brother and me felt wrong. I had friends and classmates with older siblings who described them as someone to look up to, occasionally bossy, and fiercely protective. And while my brother has many admirable qualities, I never found myself feeling protected by him or looking up to him. In fact, it was the other way around. When I had a coffee roll donut, all of a sudden his chocolate donut was unappealing. When I went across the monkey bars for the first time, he followed soon after, and he did it even better. When it came to my brother and me, I took on the role of protecting him, teaching him to distinguish between comments that can be spoken aloud in public and the ones that can be voiced only in the privacy of his room. Taking on these roles, however, doesn't change the fact that he is still two years older than I am.

The younger sibling is stereotyped as someone who needs to be babied more, can get away with more, and can feel like the center of attention. Though my parents spent a lot of time supporting me, Ian always needed it more. A compromise implies that both parties have to give something up to make the experience better for the greater good, but it can be difficult and even exhausting trying to get an eight-year-old boy with autism to agree to things that could cause a meltdown. So, that left me to get less than what my six-year-old self felt was ideal. When I was young, my parents made sure to explain that this was the reality of my family. We are our own normal.

To explain my role in my family, I often describe myself as his "older" younger sister. Many of the traditional older sibling expectations fall onto me, such as explaining the world to my brother and reaching some intellectual and educational milestones he will never even see. And yet, that doesn't change the fact that I am two years younger than him and experienced starting kindergarten, getting to sit in the front seat, and graduating high school after he did. Ian is older than I am, and yet, needed so much more than I did. So where does that put me? Well, I consider myself somewhere in the middle, maybe more toward the older side.

One of my first memories of realizing that my brother and I are not equals was when I was around seven years old. My parents decided to take us on a family cruise ship, now known as Ian's second least favorite place (it's only slightly better than forcing him to sit through a movie in the theater). After receiving the disability pass, we were able to be one of the first groups of people to enter *The Jewel*. Magnificent doesn't even begin to describe just how spectacular the ship was. Thousands of rooms, a pool and hot tub, an auditorium, all-you-can-eat buffets, the list goes on. Even with my horrific motion sickness, I was excited to explore such an intricate and stunning vessel.

As they sounded the horn and the ship was ready to depart, things started to go downhill. The sound was grilling, like the loudest car horn you could hear with an added bass layer. To say my autistic brother with heightened sensory issues didn't like this noise is a very gross understatement. His hands flew to his ears and tears streamed down his face. No one else was enjoying the noise, including me, and I also had my hands pressed hard against my ears. My parents both rushed to Ian's side and, rather than protecting their own ears, placed their hands over his ears as well to give him extra protection from the noise. Although Ian and I were both in distress, for a moment, seeing my parents run to my brother instead made me jealous. Aren't I the baby? Why would they rather help him? My jealousy subsided when I managed to look up at my brother and my parents. What I saw wasn't just another little kid bothered by the booming foghorn; I saw my brother sobbing, screaming, kicking, and physically unable to protect his ears without my parents' help. I wanted my mommy and daddy, but he **needed** them, and I realized that I was going to have to accept that crucial difference, in that moment and from then on.

As we settled on the ship, my parents started making plans about things they were going to do, many of which were adult events that Ian and I were not interested in or able to attend. When they went to these types of events, my parents dropped us off at the kids' play area. The staff members stood near the entrance to greet the kids as they walked in, with bright smiles on their faces and sea-themed name tags like "Turtle" and "Ocean". These people certainly didn't live up to their fun names, however, and made all the kids play "the quiet game" when we, a bunch of elementary school-aged kids, became too loud. Through their constant use of this silent game, it became quickly apparent that they had no idea how to handle or entertain most kids, let alone a nine-year-old boy with autism. During these silent periods, it was up to me, my brother's seven-year-old sister, to sit with him and keep his energy contained while the staff would reprimand little kids for being excited to be on a cruise.

This event was a key turning point for me, considering I still remember it about thirteen years later. The cruise was the first time I really felt like I was an older sister to my brother. I realized I was going to be taking on the older sibling role for the most part, and this was just the way it was. Part of me always wished that he could be the protective older brother who I could complain to and watch get angry with others on my behalf; however, the roles ended up being entirely switched. I felt a sense of duty to make sure that my brother was okay, which escalated during the high school years when we started going to school together.

I took pride in ensuring that people were nice to him; I grew to like playing the part of the older sister in school. This role was perfectly fine—in fact, it seemed normal until I started receiving unusual compliments.

Have you ever been complimented just for being related to someone? And no, I'm not talking about a "You're such a great sister", I'm talking about comments such as "The way you speak to your brother is truly inspirational" or "It's amazing how patient you are with him." The compliments were literally about being related to a person with a disability, even though I didn't do anything besides treat him like he's a member of my family. People glorifying our relationship may not sound offensive, and it can very well come from a well-intentioned place, but it feels disingenuous, like they're applauding my physical ability to interact with my brother, not our relationship as a whole. I'll tell you this: I don't think you would love it if you overheard someone complimenting your sibling or friend for just having a conversation with you. Can you imagine having people telling you, at 17, that it's amazing that you have the ability to converse with your 19-year-old brother?

About three years ago, when I was a senior in high school and my brother was a super senior (as per the Individuals with Disabilities Education Act[3] (IDEA), Ian was able to be in high school until he was 21 years old), we entered the school together as we did every day. Something to know about Ian is that he is one of the friendliest people I've ever known, so much so that other students would come up to me to tell me how happy he's made them. I'd give a quick thank you, but I'd try to remind them that they could, and should, be telling all of this to him, instead of just to me. He's so friendly that he would say hello to our bus driver and every teacher he passed in the morning by name. One morning, we passed by a teacher who also happened to be a Black woman. She knew Ian fairly well, but you really don't have to know him well to know that he was not ill-intentioned.

"You are a brown woman!" my brother loudly exclaimed upon seeing her. A comment that, to him, is just announcing a characteristic, while to another, it may come off as insulting. My white principal came running over.

"You're a brown woman, and our principal is a tan woman", he announced again.

You would've thought my brother just shouted an obscenity at this Black teacher because my principal looked like a deer in the headlights; she had no idea what to do. Before my principal could interject I turned to my brother.

"Ian, please look at me", I said.

He turned to look at me. I made sure I really had his attention.

"People don't like it when you comment on how they look unless it's to say that you like something. It's best to keep those thoughts to yourself."

He nodded.

"Ian, what did I just say?" I had to make sure he actually understood me.

Older-younger sister   15

"We should only talk about skin color in private, not in public", he repeated to me.

"Good. Have a good day in class!" I said to him as we parted ways.

I started to walk away myself, assuming that everything had been handled. But, before I could start to leave, my principal stepped right in front of me. She gave me this look like I had just heroically saved a kitten from a tree.

"It's so amazing to see you speak with him", she smiled at me, "How did you know just what to say to him?" she asked.

I was absolutely dumbfounded by such a question. She essentially asked me, "How do you know how to speak with your brother who you've lived with for 17 years?" It was my turn to feel like a deer caught in the headlights, as I stood there staring back at her with nothing to say. After what felt like a whole minute of having a stare-off with my principal, I eventually told her something along the lines of, "I don't know, I just do."

Think of it this way: Consider the scenario when you encounter a family with a little two-year-old girl. You go over to them to try to interact with the child and the child says something unintelligible that just sounds like a cute mumble. You have no idea what she said, but suddenly the parents chime in with a "She said that she likes your pink shirt." To you, the toddler's sentence sounds garbled, whereas the parents, who know how their child communicates, were able to translate for their kid right away. Taking this concept one step further, let's take this same two-year-old. If the child were to come up to you and shout "Where's Elsa?", what would be your first reaction? It would probably be something like, "Who is Elsa? What does she look like? Is she one of your friends?" However, in this situation, the parents of the two-year-old would say "Elsa is in Arendelle with Princess Anna, Kristoff, and Sven." The parents know that their child loves the Disney movie *Frozen*, so when she refers to Elsa, they immediately know that she's referring to Queen Elsa, and not a real person. My parents have referred to this as the "Romeo and Juliet Effect". When Juliet says, "Wherefore art thou, Romeo", it immediately evokes a sense of longing, loving, passion, and even sadness because most people have read Shakespeare's most famous play and are therefore able to contextualize just that one sentence. This is how my parents and I experienced my brother. Sometimes he blurts out complete non-sequiturs, and sometimes he makes comments about how people look, but my family and I can mostly tell what he means when he speaks, and over the years we've learned how to speak back to him in ways that make sense. This may look like speaking slowly, respectfully, more concisely, and ensuring good eye contact. It's not a miracle that I can do this—he's just my immediate family.

There are three categories of people who interact with my brother. The first category comprises people like my principal who tend to misunderstand him; these are people who are well intentioned but simply don't know how to communicate with people with disabilities or their family members without coming off as being insensitive or overly sensitive. Many times, these people will unintentionally infantilize people with autism, just as my principal did. The infantilization of people with autism takes control away from their own lives, thereby increasing their need for dependency on others, and potentially crushes their confidence to venture out socially. Second, there are those who are able to interact with people with disabilities more naturally, whether due to a personal experience or just their personality. The last, and as many would agree, is the worst category of people who lack compassion and are just mean. I use this term distinctively from "ableist", as ableism shows up in many ways—ranging from people who feel familiarity is better or more normal to those feeling awkward and uncomfortable around people with disabilities. Some people may not even realize the fact that they are ableists, or, if they do, they at least have the decency to keep it to themselves. This last category of people has offensive, outdated beliefs that judge and harm people with disabilities (Dunn, 2021).

Many years ago, my dad, Ian, and I were in line at a Starbucks to treat ourselves to coffee and donuts. I was lost in the menu, deciding between a caramel or mocha Frappuccino when I heard Ian start to laugh. Sometimes, when his brain is full of so many ideas, he just starts to laugh and think out loud. My dad and I turned to see Ian facing a girl and her boyfriend whose style I would describe as goth. My brother is not a judgmental person as he has no concept of race being anything deeper than skin color or gayness being anything deeper than just liking someone of the same gender. He lives in a world with little nuance; he doesn't try to hurt the feelings of strangers, even when he accidentally has. He comments about people, especially if they have something unique, like a bald head, round Harry Potter glasses, or an interesting clothing style, like a gothic-inspired one. The girl, who was an adult, aggressively turned to my young teenage brother and asked him what he thought was so funny. He responded, with a warm smile on his face, "You have a choker on your neck." To this, she and her boyfriend, who was just as insecure as she was, started scolding my brother and telling him to get away from her, as if he was some creepy guy hitting on her and not a teenage boy standing there flapping his hands, squealing with happiness.

"Have you ever heard of compassion?", my dad chimed in, "because you should really look into it. It might make you less miserable." Mic drop!

Others in the Starbucks turned to praise my dad, and an employee even came over to him from behind the counter to apologize for the goth girl's behavior toward someone who so very clearly didn't know any better.

Over these past few years, I have been developing a style of my own that, while certainly not goth, would fall under an alternative category. I enjoy wearing mostly black, with skulls and silver chains dangling from my ears and neck.

"You have ripped pants and big earrings", Ian will say.

"Do you like it?" I ask.

"I love it!" He says it every time without fail. He says what he thinks out loud, which for some seems to be too difficult a concept to understand.

Ian's out-loud commentary comes from a place of love and interest. As I've mentioned before, people will tell me that he's made a crummy day feel a little better. He loves going up to people and introducing himself and his family. He could go on and on about his love for his favorite TV shows, *Miraculous Ladybug* and *The Big Bang Theory*. He'll sing as loud as his tone-deaf voice will let him, and he will happily dance around like no one's watching. He is unapologetically himself, and I wish more than anything that more people saw him the way I do.

Some of his best moments are when he's able to completely unmask his autism. When asked about what my brother is like, I respond with "Ian is unable to mask his autism", meaning that you will be able to tell that he has an intellectual disability upon first interaction with him. This, however, doesn't mean that there aren't times when he has to mask by sitting still and staying silent. Masking, while unfortunately sometimes necessary, can have harmful impacts on the individual, sometimes suppressing the very personality that people on the spectrum have noticed within themselves (Miller, Rees and Pearson, 2021). One of the best environments I've seen him in is when he is able to work at my Aunt Denise's daycare/preschool. In the summer of 2023, I worked at this daycare full time and my brother would come in once a week to teach music class and help out around the building. Teaching music included singing and dancing and using drums to learn *piano*, *adagio*, *allegro*, and *prestissimo*, all terms to describe tempo in classical music that Ian can list and define off the top of his head. Ian has clung onto a lot of his interests from when he was really little, but it's appropriate for him to let this all out when he's at a daycare singing songs and talking about the things the children like to watch. My family has found that a daycare allows Ian the space to almost fully unmask and be around little kids that he absolutely loves. The kids also really enjoy having him around. Children between the ages of two and five, who are too young to know what autism is but old enough to see that he's a funny fellow, really gravitate toward him, as they see some of their silliness, creativity, imagination, and energy reflected in an adult figure.

At the daycare, a three-year-old girl once asked the staff whether Ian was different. "I love him very much", she said, "I just want to know if he's different, but I love him!" Even at the age of three, this girl knew that he was different, but made sure that no one thought that meant she didn't like him. Little kids are actually much more insightful than we give them credit for, but that's a topic in and of itself. Little kids are welcoming to an adult who has common interests, and Ian fits into this role incredibly naturally (whereas, I had to do some Paw Patrol research, a show about a couple of dogs with jobs and one little boy who work together to save the day).

It is a relief that Ian can experience an environment where he can fully express himself without feeling constrained by expectations that would traditionally fall onto an adult man. That being said, his inability to control himself and his thoughts has, at times, been hurtful and difficult to reconcile with.

The space Ian takes up, though needed, has left me feeling like a middle child, somewhere in the chasm between knowing he is my older brother with needs that are typically expected from a younger sibling. This has left me without knowing what exactly my role is, riding between the real and experienced older and younger sibling spaces. Sometimes, this dynamic can make responding to his anger and meanness unique and even challenging. His inability to conceal certain thoughts that he has can be annoying and can sometimes be hurtful. At the time of writing, Ian is 22 years old, and he has never been away from home for more than a month. It is apparent that he wants to take after his "older" younger sister and go to college. While I understand that, at 22 years old, it can be frustrating to have lived full time with your parents for your entire life, he won't just say that. He'll say something like, "No fathers, no mothers, no sisters, just the orphanage/just by myself." Or, when I am due to come home from college, he'll ask about me for days before, sometimes even gracing me with a rare text that isn't just "ok". But, once I was home, he would remember that he didn't have his own bathroom anymore and would all of a sudden start repeatedly asking me when I was going back to college. Frequent complaints like this can be hard to hear, and I know that he has certainly hurt my feelings with comments like these. When I try to explain my hurt to people, they say, "You know he loves you. You know he doesn't mean it", which is such a useless response. His love for me has nothing to do with this. Would you tell a typically developing sibling when their typically developing brother, who they are excited to see and only get to visit only a handful of times, that their brother "still loves them" and that he "just doesn't mean it" when they are hurt because their brother straight up tells them that he wants them to go back to college? While I understand that my brother isn't typically developing, it's clear as day that when he asks me over and over when it's time for me to leave he means it. He's not an idiot. Contrary to what people may think, he doesn't simply say things with no meaning.

So, how **do** you respond to a sibling of someone with autism without invalidating their feelings, but also acknowledging the differences between a brother with and without autism and how that affects the situation? Allow them to explain that the situation is different; however, it could still be hurtful. Trust me, I am painfully aware that when my brother says these things to me, it's wrong of me to lash out and get angry with him. When he says these things, it's not coming from a place of personal dislike for me, but rather a dislike for having to share again, which he's just going to have to get over. Still, it's not fun to hear him complaining about me. I wish there were ways to explain to him that what he says is hurtful. He just doesn't express empathy in the way most people do. In fact, it's hard to tell what does and doesn't invoke empathy in him sometimes, so conversations like these don't really go anywhere. A lot of the time, people with autism are stereotyped as having alexithymia (lack of emotion), but this is actually not the case. While alexithymia presents more commonly in autistic individuals than in neurotypical individuals, it also shows up more in people with eating disorders, depression, schizophrenia, and substance abuse. In my opinion, it's hard to tell when Ian feels empathy because I know that I may not be able to tell exactly when empathy is and isn't invoked in him, seeing as people with autism can express their emotions in ways neurotypical people don't always recognize (Brewer and Murphy, 2016). Still, not being able to recognize when he feels bad for hurting my feelings hurts, and hence when the sibling of a person with autism wants to vent, let them vent. Let them get their anger or sadness out because they know they can't prevent the remarks from coming. Since it can't be stopped, at least give them the space to be upset and figure out how they are going to cope with such comments. The younger sibling in me wants to be upset with him, but the older sibling knows that I need to deal with my hurt in other ways that don't involve me being mean back to him.

For many of the times Ian has hurt my feelings, I can think of ways he has shown me how special I am to him. As I mentioned, most of the time, Ian only texts the word "ok", but sometimes he'll start really having a conversation with me.

If it's not an "ok", the next thing Ian likes to text me about is one of his favorite shows, *Miraculous Ladybug*. *Miraculous Ladybug* is a French show that follows the love square of two characters, Marinette and Adrien, who, when there's a bad guy, turn into beloved superheroes, Ladybug and Cat Noir. Unaware of their identities, Marinette crushes on Adrien, and Adrien crushes on Ladybug, but they spend the majority of the show either afraid or unable to express their feelings for each other. Due to the simplicity of the plot (which, recently, has gotten less simple), Ian is able to watch and enjoy the show every Sunday morning. Ian loves assigning characters to real-life people: for example, I am Marinette/Ladybug, and he is Adrien/Cat Noir. After they defeat the bad guys, the two heroes always end with the punchline "Pound It!" as they fist bump each other. When this happens, Ian and I do the fist bump after they do, and, throughout the episode, Ian makes sure I don't miss any of my dialogues, such as the line Marinette says when turning into Ladybug, or the one she quotes when calling upon her power, the "Lucky Charm". Ian has bought us each matching plushies, action figures, books, and even custom pajama sets for this show. Seeing him get so deep into something that he specifically likes doing with me demonstrates the fact that I will always be special to him, no matter how many times he complains about having a sibling to share with.

Because of our special relationship, it made me sad that, up until high school, we didn't go to school together because they didn't have a program suited for Ian. My school was so underprepared in how to support students with autism that, when I started kindergarten my school put me in the special education classroom, assuming that, after my brother, that's where I would need to go. Fortunately, this problem was quickly solved, but Ian continued at a different school until ninth grade, after he repeated eighth grade. His out-of-district teachers supported him well, and he actually learned the least while he was in secondary education. My parents spoke highly of his teachers but explained that high-quality teachers are not as common as they should be. Aside from the fact that my elementary and middle school didn't even have a program for him, a lot of the time, the programs that do exist are ridden with issues. After witnessing Ian's educational journey firsthand and watching him not being able to go to school in the town he lived in, I knew that I wanted to make a difference. Advocacy and education go hand in hand, and I want to advocate for those who are unable to do this for themselves by being their educator and giving them the tools and opportunities that will help them achieve this. More schools should have better special education programs, as it is important for these students to not be isolated from but welcomed into their community that, for many, is mostly done through the school district. Classes, clubs, sports, trips, all of these things are done with other kids in school, but Ian wasn't able to do this in his own community. Once he came back to our district and was in stage crew, gym, and art with typically developing students, I quickly became known as "Ian's sister" by students other than those in my grade while he was getting recognized outside of school in the community he belongs in. The reason he wasn't able to be included in his own district was not because of him, but due to the fact my school lacked a program and educators that were good enough to help him. No child is a burden to education, and this message should translate through public schools offering better quality education for students with disabilities, which is exactly what I want to do.

There's a lot to say about what makes my and everyone's relationships with Ian unique to how we experience relationships with neurotypical people. That being said, I think I've gone on enough about everything that makes our relationship different. While I acknowledge that every relationship is unique, my relationship with Ian is, in fact, like no other. Because of our perceived different relationship, I've found that some people will infantilize him. As noted earlier, people approach me before going to him to say something about him, assuming that he's incapable of engaging with them. But, what people tend not to realize is that Ian is a lot like everyone else in many ways. Ian loves pop music, including artists like Taylor Swift, Ke$ha, Katy Perry, Doja Cat, and Harry Styles. Sometimes, if I pick him up from an activity or take him to his weekly bowling events, I'll queue songs that we both know and we'll sing along together in the front seat. He has always loved songs and music, so much so that he taught music to a group of preschoolers once a week. It's unfortunate how tone-deaf he is (he's unable to match pitch) because music is one of his favorite things to talk about, next to families. He talks about girls that he thinks are pretty and how he could have a wife one day. Since I started talking about going to college, he has become interested in being able to live independently in a college-like environment. Over the years, he has had several career ideas, like being a bus driver, a chef, and a preschool teacher, the latter of which he has already dabbled in. I hope, despite the difficulties he faces and the government limitations on the money he can receive if he has a job, that he will be able to pursue something that makes him happy. Ian has autism, and this makes him different, but this does not change the fact that he's a 22-year-old man who wants a life just like anyone else. In the last few years, autism has become less stigmatized and diagnoses have been increasing. Parents of children with disabilities in particular deflect back against those who push stigmas, challenging these bigoted mindsets by using resistant strategies (Manago, Davis and Goar, 2017). This makes me hope for a world that caters better to people who aren't the majority, for example, making scissors for left-handed people. Inclusion in schools is increasing with research saying that inclusion builds compassion and allows students with disabilities access to peers their age and grade level content. If this concept could translate into the "real world" allowing for opportunities for Ian, he could finally have a taste of the "normalcy" he sometimes longs for. I've never met anyone else like my brother, and I hope that the world embraces him the way a sister would embrace her brother.

Reflective questions

1. How can you support siblings of people with disabilities?

2. What are the three typical ways in which people interact with people with disabilities?

   a. Which way shows loving interactions toward others? How does it show love?

3. What is masking? How did masking affect Ian? How does it affect people with disabilities at large?

4. Why do you think the term "normalcy" is in quotation marks?

3
Mama Bear

Millie Rodríguez

In the spring of 2009, I sat in the assistant principal's office at my child's school to discuss why my third grader with autism would not be included in the "REACH" gifted program. Despite earning an above-average score on the IQ test and their teachers recognizing them as academically advanced, my child (who now identifies as nonbinary) was ineligible for the enrichment REACH provided because their scores on parts of the IQ test were not above average (processing speed and communications, of course) and because they were already receiving speech therapy services. I pushed back and told the assistant principal that I had been reading up on this, and I wanted to formally request that they retest with the Raven's test since it works better for children with limited communication skills or for children who are nonverbal. She looked at me and said,

"Wouldn't that be playing to his strengths?"

I was incredulous and responded, "So, it's ok to play to his weaknesses?"

She was not expecting that and simply said, "Well, that's not a test we offer here, but you are welcome to get the test at your own expense and share the results."

Being the sole income provider in my family, and on a teacher's salary no less, that was not going to happen. I knew from that day forward that I would have to be a fierce advocate for my child, which came naturally to me, but made me the "angry Latina mom" to them. Thankfully, I was a teacher and co-taught inclusion classes throughout my career. Not many other parents have that advantage and access to knowledge or social capital (Yosso, 2005). Social capital in this context means I had what my parents and so many parents of children with disabilities didn't while raising their children—a network of professional colleagues who became loving, supportive friends who were able to help me understand special education and help direct my next steps. When I didn't understand what I read or what my options were, my social network pulled through.

Looking back, I get so angry because what was the point of denying opportunities for growth to a clearly talented child? My child, though they didn't meet one specific area criteria, could obviously benefit from enrichment opportunities. Administrators and teachers claim to want involved parents, but when some families **do** get involved and are knowledgeable, they are deemed too needy, too pushy, and too demanding (Flores Martin, 2022; Lalvani and Hale, 2015). This was true in my experience. I was treated as if I were asking too much, as if I were unreasonable, and as if what I was asking for was idealistic and not realistic, but my love for my child and my hopes and dreams would not let me let up. I often sit and wonder whether the administrator involved ever reflects and wishes they knew then what they know now…IF they have even grown in their understanding of Autism Spectrum Disorder (ASD) and neurodivergence (ND).

Discovering a new calling

That was not the first or last time I was denied reasonable requests for my child, but I know many may wonder about our backstory. First, one day recently my children and I were having a conversation about the controversy around mercury in vaccinations causing ASD, and even though there is no thimerosal used anymore, there are still parents who refuse to vaccinate their children. I don't care what people say causes autism because *I* know it's a natural part of neurodiversity. What was (and is) more important to me was how I would support my child in realizing their goals in life. However, my child with autism said something very profound: "When I hear about people saying they're not allowing their child to get vaccinated because they don't want them to get autism, all I hear is that they don't want a kid like me."

My pregnancy was normal; my child passed the Apgar. They were jaundiced and needed a few days under blankets and lights, but other than that, everything seemed fine. After a while, I noticed that although they were a happy baby, they didn't like snuggling. They would not look at me, and even when I would nurse, they tugged at me, so they didn't have to look at me. The mommas out there know that this is how the love bond is reinforced, and it did concern me. As they began to grow, their communication seemed delayed; there were no typical verbalizations or indications of what they might need when they were crying. They were slow to walk, but once they did, they toddled happily and loved running to and from the oven door looking at their reflection and laughing at the baby they saw. They didn't respond to their name or noise, but they passed their hearing test…and they laid

32   Love is Praxis

their body on the glider ottoman…and rocked and rocked and rocked. I knew in my heart that there was something different, but I had no idea what. I talked to the pediatrician, and she told me I was comparing them to their older sister, and that biologically male babies often develop slower than biologically female babies. I understood that. I had read all that, but I **lived** with my baby. I knew it was something else. She encouraged me to get in touch with Easter Seals in case I felt strongly about it, but she was sure nothing would turn up. I did call, and they came to our home for an evaluation. My baby was 17 months old by this time, and my child wasn't walking as much as before. I had read that it might be a temporary regression due to a recent move to a new home. In addition, although they started making some sounds, they still were not communicating, and we often didn't know what they needed or why they were crying. From the evaluation, I learned that my child had a fine and gross motor delay and was developmentally delayed in their speech and joint attention, which is critical to communication. They started occupational therapy (OT), physical therapy (PT), and speech therapy almost immediately. They soon met all their goals for PT and were toddling around again. However, they were still struggling with talking, spatial reasoning, and executive functioning, so they continued with speech and OT, particularly to address their sensory processing dysfunction.

One afternoon in 2003, my mom called and told me to hurry up and turn on Oprah. She said they were talking about this thing called autism, and the behaviors described sounded just like my baby. We watched together while staying on the phone, and I was in shock. A lot of what they were saying—rocking, meltdowns, lining up toys, not talking, not responding to their name—were all behaviors my child exhibited…could my child be **disabled**? The next time their speech therapist came to the house, I asked her what she thought. She said she was not allowed to say. I redirected and asked her if it were her child, would she get them evaluated for autism? She shook her head yes. I asked her where she would go, and she said she would go to either Hershey[4] or Kennedy Kreiger, and she would get on the waiting list six months before their birthday. That's what I did.

Soon after their third birthday, we went to Hershey, and the evaluation confirmed our suspicion: Pervasive Development Disorder-Not Otherwise Specified (PDD-NOS), or, colloquially, High Functioning Autism (HFA). I was happy to have a diagnosis that would open doors to therapies, but at the same time, as any other parent/caregiver whose child has just received a diagnosis knows, I was afraid. Would my child have a normal life? Now, before anyone starts bashing my language, that was the language I used in 2004 before I knew better. I immediately threw myself into all kinds of autism research in order to gain a deeper understanding. I made calls, attended meetings and professional development workshops, participated in a meeting to create an Individualized Family Services Plan[5] (IFSP), learned to navigate case management, as well as connected with an agency that provided a Behavioral Specialist Consultant (BSC) and Therapeutic Support Staff (TSS). Almost all of my Act 48 professional development hours (a requirement for teachers to maintain their certification in Pennsylvania) were autism related. When my child turned five and started school, I asked for an Individualized Education Plan[6] (IEP), but since my child performed well on the kindergarten readiness test, they were eligible only for the occupational therapy and speech therapy they were already getting. I agreed because, even with all I was learning, I didn't know better—yet. I was also learning about how autism manifested in my child. They loved their half-day kindergarten class, but the noise, lights, the sometimes rowdy children (as is expected in kindergarten), and long hours caused them to experience sensory overload and have a meltdown every afternoon. I also learned that my child was very rules-bound, so the other children not following directions caused an enormous amount of inner turmoil. Instead of being understanding of my child's needs, the teacher asked us to work with them on their tattling. I had to start advocating for my child's needs since I now realized that my love for my child drove me to learn about how to adjust to meet their needs. But this was not their child, and due to the teacher's and administrator's lack of education around autism, and because of my child's intellectual abilities, they expected my kindergartner to behave like a "typical" student.

"No" is a choice

We requested the agency we were working with to assign the TSS school hours to help my child with their self-regulation and tattling. Soon, they were doing so well in school that the teacher and administrators communicated to me that they wanted the TSS to stop coming to school. Their reason was that the TSS made my child stand out from the rest and that my child was doing well. I said, "Don't you think they are successful **because** the TSS is there?" I got so aggravated by this that I told my child to have meltdowns in school if they were feeling overwhelmed instead of waiting until they got home. I believe that was the turning point in my relationship with the school personnel because the TSS told the teacher what I said, after which the teacher emailed me and cc'd the assistant principal. After that, no matter what I went in to meet with them about, I faced an immovable wall of ignorance, bias, and smugness. I was treated as inferior, as if they knew special ed law better than I did, which was probably true at the time. They put barriers before me like not allowing me to meet with the principal because the assistant principal was the one who dealt with these types of issues. Out of desperate love for my child, I went to see the assistant principal again the summer just before first grade started. I had just come back from the National Autism Conference at Penn State and learned about buddy systems. I wanted that for my child. I laid out what I learned and how effective it seemed to be, and she told me my child wasn't "disabled enough" to warrant needing a buddy system. She said that they got along fine with their classmates in kindergarten, and besides, kids don't notice if another student is "quirky". Quirky.

I told her, "Not yet, but they will, and my child will need friends to support them."

She finally said, "That is too much to ask a child and a family."

Even when I told her that I already had a family who was willing and that all she needed to do was to make sure both our children were always in the same class from here on out, and maybe try to recruit other families, she still refused. She said that I could talk to families and talk to them about their children, but that she could not ensure that any group of children could be placed together

36   Love is Praxis

in the same class year after year. After being at the autism confer-ence and seeing examples of school districts that did it for stu-dents who were now ten years older than my child, I knew this was not impossible. I knew her "no" was a choice.

So, can you guess what happened as a result of a "no buddy sys-tem" when my child was dysregulated on full school days and started having meltdowns in school and was unable to com-municate why? The administration called my oldest child from her classroom to ask what was wrong with her sibling. What was an eight-year-old supposed to do? What happened when there was no buddy system when, in third grade, my child found that vestibular regulation helped them get through the school day? A group of girls started teasing and calling my child gay because they were biologically male and loved being on the swings at recess. Somehow, in third grade, these young students were already engaging in a gender norming practice that says swings were a girl activity instead of an activity that all children can enjoy. Because my child didn't have a buddy group, it took months for them to pay attention to the faces of the students say-ing those things and recognize one enough to associate a name. It felt like months of me afterward talking to the same assistant principal about it because she didn't believe that a student, a very sweet and gentle child overall, could ever say such a thing. The administrator did nothing, which resulted in me approach-ing the girl's mom myself. The mom, too, was incredulous, but guess what stopped happening when I went Mama Bear on that mom? Unfortunately, it was temporary. Bullying from other students started again in fourth grade. With my child having nothing to look forward to at school except bullying, fluorescent lights, and overwhelming ambient noise, they became a child who screamed and cried and wouldn't get out of the vehicle in the drop-off lane, a child who had to be carried into school kicking and writhing in pain from the grip of the PE teacher. There was a reprieve in fifth grade when they finally found a classmate who was happy to be their buddy and protector. However, there was still no official buddy system in place, and you don't want to guess what happened. Even after begging for that best friend, buddy, and protector from fifth grade to **please** be placed with them in sixth grade, the school refused to honor the request. During sixth grade, my child, only 11 years old, verbalized suicidal ideation and made an attempt because of the incessant bullying.

I continued to learn more about autism myself and tried to educate my colleagues and my child's educators. I explained self-regulation, visual schedules, task chains, and so on—all of which are part of the elementary classroom but needed to be implemented more explicitly with my child with ASD. Though autism was a buzzword and everyone was frightened and intrigued by it, the education system was slow to move to support students with the diagnosis. Because of the educational system's ignorance of neurodivergence, students like mine were placed on more rigid behavior management programs. The worst part was that students would lose any progress with just one meltdown because teachers and administrators failed to realize that the meltdown was a manifestation of their disability—namely, their inability to self-regulate. It was a no-win situation.

I also remember when my child was in fifth grade, though I had fought tooth and nail to keep them in speech therapy, they were released from their IEP. They met all of their speech goals, and the school decided not to provide them with social communication skills because it did not affect their academic achievement. There was a social skills club that my child didn't particularly like because it was with students who were explosive and "mean". In addition, the gifted teacher had just changed, and when I asked this new educator early in the year to not talk to my child about how "lucky" they were to be so skinny, my child stopped being invited to the enrichment meetings that the previous gifted educator had been gracious enough to do. Current research suggests that the best way to prepare students with autism for college is to build on their strengths and provide enrichment opportunities that will help them improve their areas of growth, like communication and executive functioning (Austermann *et al.*, 2023). The school and the gifted educator not understanding the meaning of twice exceptional and not meeting the needs of an academically talented and inquisitive child because of certain parts of an IQ test was a failure on their part. On all accounts, my child didn't stop needing support—they needed the IEP to change to meet their developmental needs.

In 2014, we moved to a new school district in Pennsylvania, and I was so excited because we were in the same county as a large, well-respected higher education institution—the schools HAD to be better. I scheduled a meeting with the administrators to talk about my children, meaning my middle child's diagnosis and my other two children who had Gifted Individualized Education Plans[7] (GIEPs). Neither of the GIEPs was carried over, and when I asked to speak with my middle child's teachers to tell them about how autism presents for them, the principal said that wasn't necessary, but that I could email the teachers individually. When I asked whether I could present a talk to the students in that grade (about 130 students) about what autism is, how it presents, and how they can support their new classmate, I was told that was very irregular and unnecessary. When I shared our history, explaining that my child was the target of bullies at their previous school, the principal simply said bullying wasn't an issue in their school. Within one semester, my child was quickly identified as "different" and became a target again, so much so that by tenth grade the whole football team was tormenting my child.

I talked to the administration at the high school about what I saw and what my child told me, and I was made to feel delusional. The principal didn't think there was any way the football players were doing that. Most of them volunteered in the self-contained classroom and were supportive of students with disabilities.

"But do they know that my student has a disability?"

"No, not unless someone told them."

"My point exactly. My kid is just a weirdo to them, and they are being bullies."

I had been substituting as much as possible at that school just to try to support my child since nobody else would. I remember walking down the hall behind my child who was crouching their body—trying so hard to not be seen—when one of the football players with a Napoleon complex came around a corner and jumped up and swung his arm over my child's shoulder. I couldn't hear what he was saying, but I taught middle and high school for 14 years. I knew body language. I called out for him to get off my child.

"What? We're best friends, aren't we?" he said, looking at my child.

"Funny…as you know, that's my kid, and they never talk about you", I said. "Get. Off. Of. Them."

This bullying caused my child to regress to the point of crying under their desk **in high school**, and one day when I was trying to get them into my car to go to school, they verbalized suicidal ideation, saying they would do it. I did what I had to do. I called the Crisis Center and had them admitted. It was the worst day of my life because at the center later that night, after forgetting to inspect my child's jeans for a belt even though they took the string from their hoodie, my child wrapped the belt around their neck and tightened as much as possible in their despair, and was found on their bed. I heard the fear in the director's voice when he called to warn me that I might see some bruising the next day. For the next several days, my child pleaded to come home. To see them walk into the visitation room, shoulders hunched, with hopeful smiles, and scared eyes, it took everything not to break down in tears each time. They told me about the noises and lights that bothered them and that they couldn't sleep well. They told me about the kids screaming at each other in therapy. They told me about the girl cussing and throwing a chair across the room. When I told the director that this didn't seem the appropriate placement for someone on the spectrum, he agreed that it was not, but disagreed with my request to discharge my child. By the end of the first week, because that placement was **not** appropriate for someone with ASD, I signed my child out early against medical advice.

All along, the high school continued to believe it was not the bullying that caused the meltdowns but my child's desire to avoid the tasks set forth, as proven by a Functional Behavior Analysis (FBA). However, as many researchers know, you see what you want to see (Kida, 2006). Most of the time, the crawling under the desk was in the same class as that football player from the hall. I don't even want to imagine what happened to provoke that behavior almost every day in that class. There was another teacher, who I loved and was great for my older child, who said my middle child was capable but was just lazy and manipulating me. To this day, I can still feel the frenetic feelings I had when this teacher said that to me, and I have to consciously regulate my breathing and emotions because remembering it makes me want to go around with a baseball bat, destroying everything in sight. Like I said, I am Mama Bear. My love for my child became my praxis, and I was not successful in educating these "professionals". I was either the unreasonable mom or the angry Latina or both to them. They never took me seriously.

Tale of two heroes

Thankfully, after almost two years of advocacy, the school district acquiesced and gave us an IEP for Emotional/Behavioral Disturbance (EBD), and my child was allowed to enroll in a Cisco Networking program at the local vo-tech4. In reality, it was probably to shut me up, but it was the best thing they ever did up to that point. My child was still crying under the desk, but the special educator really cared for their well-being and worked hard with the classroom teachers to meet my child's needs. For example, he didn't bat an eye when I asked for chunking to be included in the IEP, which received a lot of pushback from the teachers when I initially requested it before the IEP. Chunking is when an educator breaks down large tasks into smaller units to reduce the demand on input, working memory, and processing speed (Ewing, 2024). This helped with writing assignments, and I am so grateful to the special educator for including it, even though I often had to reach out to the teachers to remind them to chunk their large assignments.

Because the bullying did not stop, my child and I had a long conversation. They didn't think they could survive another year. I decided that maybe I could move into another school district's area. I asked them what they thought of going to a new school their senior year. They too thought it was a good idea, but **only** if they could continue attending their vo-tech program. It was decided—they would go to school somewhere where nobody knew them, have a fresh start, and, hopefully, at least one year free of torment. I packed and moved because until I had that lease, I could not enroll my child. Prior to moving though, I spoke off the record with a guidance counselor about my child continuing at vo-tech as a condition of their IEP. The counselor said that would probably be allowed. Unfortunately, after completing the enrollment paperwork, the school district decided not to allow my child to continue with their part-time placement at vo-tech, even with an IEP, because the district could provide all the same courses on their campus. If you know about students with ASD, change is ridiculously hard, and the only solace my child had in switching schools for their senior year was being able to continue in the safe space created by their CISCO networking teacher at vo-tech. It was just too much. The fact that my child would rather spend their senior year at the same school knowing the treatment they would receive from ill-adjusted peers just so they could continue in vo-tech[8] with this educator tells you what a godsend he was; he was the best thing to happen to my child. He showed my child love through his educator praxis, so my child decided to continue in the school they didn't want to go to, simply to be heard, seen, validated, and celebrated by this person who became their hero.

Next steps

While trying to support my child's social and mental health, I started to get emails about transition planning. It was not something I was familiar with, and the emails just said we had to start. It didn't explain anything about what it is. Please understand that I was experiencing battle fatigue by this point because I was also trying to support the educational needs of my other two children as well in a school that seemingly did not want to go above and beyond for any students, especially mine. An old colleague of mine had told me once that the squeaky wheel gets the oil, so make noise. I had been noisy, I had been a thorn in their side, and I was tired. When I finally had the capacity to look up what transition planning meant, I emailed the special educator and said, "OK, I'm ready to come in for a meeting." This was definitely something my child needed. We were looking at colleges, and though my child had never been away from me except for one week at overnight camp in fifth grade, they were hesitantly excited about going to college. They knew my hopes were for them to attend college, and they received a letter of interest from one that had a Game Sciences program. We met and the special educator told me that we had to start planning for what they would do after high school, and whether or not they would stay in school until they were 21. I told her college was in the plan, and so no, they wouldn't be in high school until they were 21. I then asked in what ways they prepared students to transition to life after high school. She informed me that they take the students on field trips to the laundromat to learn how to do laundry, to the grocery store to go food shopping, to McDonald's to learn how to order food, and how to count change so they make sure they get the right amount back. I was angry once again. Had she not even read my child's IEP? I will admit that I was rude when I said, "They have a 131 IQ! They know how to do laundry, count money, and order at a restaurant! How are you going to get them ready for **college**? They need to learn self-advocacy, time management, social skills…" She looked at me baffled and said, "Oh…we don't do that here."

In the fall of 2019, without any transition services, my child went to Rensselaer Polytechnic Institute[9] (RPI), a college located in Troy, NY. I already knew about the difference between entitlement and eligibility in higher education. I had been working in higher ed for two years, so I also knew about the Family Education Rights and Privacy Act[10] (FERPA). I was scared witless because FERPA meant that there were limits to what I could know and how I could intercede on my child's behalf. Imagine, if you will, dropping your child five hours away, where the only people who knew about their disability was the Disability Resource Office, where they would only get help if they asked for it. Self-advocacy is not an autistic child's strong suit. Also imagine that the whole time you are supposed to be happy, but you are worried because you know that part of their disability presentation is the isolating inability to interact smoothly socially. You also remember that they experienced suicidal ideation twice before, and they wished they had been successful. After a lengthy "see you later", you return to your car, pull around in front of their building, and text them to come to their window, and you and your other two children wave frantically at them. They are only a shadow in that room, no light, but you can see their silhouette and their hand up, not waving, just up, and you know that **anything** could happen—anything. Every single fear was in my throat and pouring out of my eyes. Every fall, parents tearfully drop off their children at college, but only the very few leave crying because they are wondering if their child with a disability (or mental illness) will be okay or if it will be too much and their child will finally be successful in wanting the pain to end.

For a family that experienced this, FERPA is the worst thing in American education, and with so many students with disabilities now attending college, it is something that should be revisited and have new provisions built in. I had to call the police twice to my child's university to have a well-check. That was aside from the times I reached out to residence life to have their RA check in on them and tell them to call home. The second time I called RPI police was in February 2020, just about a month after dropping them off and hearing the RA admit she hadn't seen them in at least two weeks, despite them being next-door neighbors in the residence hall.

Some people say spring of 2020 and the pandemic were the worst things to happen to them or the world. It was the best thing to happen to me; when I picked up my child from RPI in March because of the pandemic, they admitted on the way home the only reason they were sitting next to me was because they knew I was coming soon to pick them up, and they didn't want me to be the one to find them. They didn't have to explain. I knew what they meant.

The way forward

We need to do better in education to support our neurodivergent students, especially those who are twice exceptional and want to lead fulfilling lives. We need to stop imposing our ideas of success and lead with the student's strengths. We need to grow their talents and provide enrichment opportunities that challenge them. We need to explicitly teach self-determination and self-advocacy. Transition planning in high school needs to accommodate students with disabilities who want to attend college and provide appropriately challenging transition planning for those who do not. I am pursuing my PhD because love is my praxis. For 17 years I've been made to feel like I was unreasonable, asking too much, and didn't know what I was talking about. I don't want any other parent to go through what I did. Special educators need to better understand students and families like mine, so they can support the students in realizing their own determinants of success, not what society tells them success looks like. We need to revise IDEA and FERPA to allow parent advocates for students with a documented disability.

My child finally felt like they could attempt college again when they turned 21 years old. It's been a year and a half now, and they are slowly (i.e. part-time) studying Information Sciences and Technology with a concentration in networking and are finding it to be a good pace for them. They once said that they felt like they were a disappointment for not going to college and finishing on time. I told them they could never disappoint me and who says we have to listen to society's timeline of in at 18, out in four years? Why do we do this to our children? Working in higher ed, I saw so many students suffering under the four-year in/out expectation. I'm happy my child is working at their own pace in a program that will lead them to achieve the goals and dreams they've set for themselves.

Reflective questions

1. What experiences have shaped your calling?
2. What are some ways you can say yes to supporting neuro-divergent students?
3. When have you been a hero to a student or child?
4. How do you visualize higher education for students with disabilities?
5. How is love showing up in your practice?

4
It's Complicated

Dana Patenaude

Families are extremely complex systems. They don't exist in a vacuum. Everyone and everything people come into contact with affects them in one way or another. As a practitioner, teacher, or professional, you will greatly impact the families you support. This is the story of my first experience with a very complicated, strong, and loving family. I had the honor of growing as a practitioner while supporting this family for approximately four years at a small clinic in a midwestern state in the US. My goal in telling this story is to inform future practitioners and teachers of the deep complexities of family relationships and the inevitable highs and lows you will face. This chapter emphasizes that despite any adversity in a therapeutic relationship, the love that a practitioner feels for a child is ever-present and weaves its way intricately into each game played, song sung, and new skill gained. Hardship within the complex relationship between a family and a practitioner does not mean there is an absence of love and care—quite the opposite. Fighting for someone demonstrates caring that cannot be found with indifference, and love is at the heart of caring for a person. Like fingerprints or snowflakes, each family is different, because of the profoundly different contexts and experiences each individual has in the family unit. I hope this story can demonstrate how working with families is beautiful, chaotic, heartbreaking, and, overall, deeply complex.

Let me introduce you to Molly. Molly (a pseudonym I created for the privacy of the family) was a three-year-old spunky little girl when I met her. Molly loved singing and dancing, climbing anything and everything, and playing with her siblings. Molly was diagnosed with autism spectrum disorder at age two. Molly lived with her mother, Amanda; and father, Andrew; grandmother; and two other siblings, Corey and Ben, also diagnosed with autism spectrum disorders. Amanda was, and I'm sure still is, a fierce advocate, like a lion protecting her cubs at all costs. She was young and funny, but a little frazzled, which was understandable with the hectic and exciting life she lives. I was so excited to work with Molly when I accepted my job as a behavior technician. Molly was one of my first clients when I first started, and she would be the client I supported for the longest amount of time. I was in my boss's office when she offered me the job on a snowy January morning. Once she offered me the job, she opened her office door and said, "That little cutie will be one of yours!" I glanced out into the playroom, where I saw a little blonde firecracker with Barbie dolls in her hands and crooked pigtails in her hair. I was blissfully and ignorantly unaware of all that we would go through together over the course of our four years together.

The first few months I spent long hours with Molly, primarily working on communication and play. When we started working together, Molly was using one-word responses to express her wants and needs but not yet engaging in reciprocal interactions. She would say things like, "Want color", "McDonald's fries?" and, most notably at this time, "NO!" She used an augmentative and alternative communication (AAC) device to support her expressive language, though she didn't have it with her consistently nor did she always want to use it when it did arrive at the clinic with her. I was new to the field of Applied Behavioral Analysis (ABA), and at this point in my career, everything was new and exciting. Although I had not had much experience with AAC devices yet, I was eager to learn. I worked hard to get to know the family as best as I could. I wasn't well versed on best practices yet, but I knew innately that it was important to me to take the time to learn about the family in order to truly know them. I also wanted to show them how dedicated I was to Molly and supporting their family. At this time, I believe they genuinely felt how much I cared about them. I consider this time a **high** and only **mildly complex**, as I was so motivated to learn. However, learning the ins and outs of a family is inherently complex. We can never truly know everything about a family, but we can work hard to know what they are willing to share with us. I now recognize this to be a component of cultural humility, which involves continuously questioning personal biases and experiences that may prohibit someone from doing their best to continue to know a family (Khan, 2021).

When I first started working with Molly's family, Amanda told me a story about their experience with a physician directly after Molly received the diagnosis of autism. She told a painful story about how the family was told to institutionalize Molly at a very young age because she would never walk, talk, or have a good quality of life. Boy were they wrong! I cried thinking about this sweet little girl never getting to play with her brothers in their backyard, or dressing up for Halloween, or singing her little heart out to

Alicia Keys. The words of professionals sting, and their impacts never quite fade, despite the years of work to prove them wrong. Thankfully, Molly proved them **so** wrong.

Moving through our years together, Molly and I hit our first significant bump. Molly began hitting, kicking, and spitting at me and other people at the clinic. Her behaviors escalated, and she was often engaging in behaviors that were dangerous to herself and others, including some of the other children. Most of the time, however, these behaviors were directed at me. There was no clear reason as to why this was happening. I was new, but even my supervisors had a hard time figuring out the reason for this out-of-the-blue escalation. Unfortunately, because I was so fresh and inexperienced then, I took this personally. I **loved** my days with Molly. I looked forward to coming to work. I couldn't fathom why she was so angry at me. Did I do something wrong? Did she hate coming to the clinic? She wasn't able to tell me at this point in her journey, so perhaps I will never know.

As a team, Molly's family and her practitioners began working on potty training with Molly during this time. Her parents shared with us that at a previous clinic in another state, Molly had been exposed to intensive potty training. They noted that the professionals conducting the intervention decided that the best method for Molly was to sit her on the toilet and keep her there until she voided. Although this method may be successful for some children, this scarred Molly deeply. When we started working on potty training at our clinic, our first step was to wave to the bathroom door in passing. She was terrified. With a lot of time and practice, we worked up to Molly being able to come into the bathroom and sit on the toilet for a few seconds! This was a huge accomplishment. Potty training was an important goal for Molly's family, and they were doing their best at home. I will emphasize, however, that this took a great deal of practice! Molly would make a great deal of progress at home but then suddenly regress, refusing to go anywhere near the toilet. It felt like one step forward, two steps back at times. However, Molly powered through it.

On one of our most trying days, Molly said something to me that got me through all of the difficult times we had been through and the challenges to come. We were in the bathroom when Molly began having a hard time coping with our potty-training routine. The same hitting, kicking, and spitting came but at an even more escalated level. She was doing things she had never done before. Again, it seemed so personal to me, but I now believe it probably wasn't. I was doing my best to calm her down and keep us both safe. However, I was feeling defeated, and I was completely alone. Just when I was ready to give up, unsure how to continue, Molly stopped. She sat down on the floor, looked at me and said, "I love you." She said this in a sad, deflated tone of voice. She had never said this to me or any member of our staff before. All of those negative feelings I had that she hated me and that this was all my fault subsided for just a few moments. I asked her if she wanted a hug, to which she said, "Yes." We hugged, completed our potty-training routine, and went back out to play. What goes down in the books as one of our toughest days together was also one I remember fondly. I took the high within the low.

Amanda and Andrew were happy to hear her expressing her emotions with her words and apologized for the bathroom dilemma. I reassured them that this was nothing to be sorry about, and that was why I was here. I didn't think then about what it must have been like for her parents to feel like they had to apologize for their daughter having such a hard day. It wasn't their fault or even hers for that matter. As a practitioner who is in fight or flight mode for a significant portion of your day, it can be really easy to forget that your hard days probably result from someone else's hardest.

Personally, I had an emotional reaction to being met with aggressive behavior so frequently during this time with Molly. I ended up having to work through the difficult experience of the reemergence of some dark memories sparked by Molly's behaviors. This was a **low** for me. However, Molly's emergence through this difficult time and facing such challenging behaviors helped me work through my own repressed memories. I learned at this point that kids change, and behaviors fluctuate. Autism is complicated, as are all children. Sometimes when a kid is giving you a hard time, it is because **they are having** a hard time. Not because of you or because of their parents. It is not always your fault **or** the family's fault.

Shortly after this storm, flowers grew within Molly. She began making strides in her communication! She was using her AAC device, an iPad with an app called Proloquo, frequently, still expressing mostly needs and wants. With the help of her AAC device, Molly was also finding her voice. This was so powerful to witness for me, a new practitioner. Our team was working really hard to help her build her communication skills, but Molly was the one working the hardest. Not only was she having success, but she was also enjoying her wins. She breezed through her work, played with passion, and continuously filled the room with laughter, day after day. I was absolutely thrilled. This accomplishment for Molly felt like an accomplishment for me, too. We were both feeling rewarded for our hard work! It was special to experience that alongside Molly and her family. Her parents were seeing such progress at home during this time as well. Her dad joked with us about how, out of all of his kids, Molly was the sweetest and was always ready to cuddle. He shared how now she was able to ask for cuddles and hugs. She even started talking back to them and giving them attitude, which they had mixed feelings about. They told silly stories of Molly copying a curse word after which Amanda or Andrew would comment, "Who knows where she heard that from!" However, they told these stories with smiles on their faces. I can only imagine how important it was for them to have these stories to tell. I often teared up at the stories they shared with me. In addition, all of her home notes from her teachers were positive with dinosaur and Paw Patrol[11] stickers (Molly's favorites). This time was definitely a high for everyone! Though times were challenging, and the work was complex, Molly was making incredible progress.

With highs come lows. The holiday season was suddenly upon us, which always came with scheduling complexities. Many families took time off, especially between Christmas and New Year's, to visit family or just spend uninterrupted time together. Many behavior technicians were in graduate school, and so they also took some time off to go see family, since they weren't typically able to do so during the semesters. This also applied to me as I was getting my master's degree during this time. I hated taking time off of work so much that I notoriously showed up to work

56   Love is Praxis

sick instead of taking off (pre-COVID times). However, I had a few weeks off of school and hadn't gotten to spend time with my family in a while.

Because I was close with Molly's family, instead of just taking off the time I wanted, I approached them with the idea of working out together when they were planning on taking time off so that we could coordinate and maximize Molly, Corey, and Ben's therapy time. For the very first time, I was met with backlash from them. They were very steadfast that they were not taking any time off, beyond when the clinic was closed, which was Christmas Day and New Year's Day only. I told them that I understood, but I did plan on taking some time off to travel back home to see my family. I told them that I wasn't sure what days I would be absent yet, but that I would let them know as soon as I knew. For the first time, they weren't as understanding as I anticipated. I thought to myself that they must have been just having one of those days because, by this point, I felt like I knew them well; I understood their moods and the reasons behind their sometimes-short responses. We spent moments in parking lots, way past the end of sessions crying together. We had a pretty solid relationship.

Things were different this time, and I was becoming concerned. This initial conversation happened at drop-off, so Molly and I said our goodbyes to her parents, and we went inside to have our session. During the session, my boss came out of her office and approached me about an email she received from Amanda. She said that our cancellation policies were unheard of and inappropriate. In her email, she didn't name me specifically, but she complained openly about her displeasure with the behavior technicians' ability to take time off from work.

As pick-up time closely approached, I was growing more and more nervous to see Amanda again, knowing the heated email she had sent. As a people-pleaser, I hated feeling like I was the reason for someone's hardships. Though I felt like I wasn't doing anything wrong, clearly she disagreed. Amanda knocked on the door a few minutes early for pick-up, which was already unusual. She stormed inside, infuriated. Her email didn't even begin to match the tone she arrived with that afternoon. I attempted to debrief Molly's session with her to tell her how wonderful of a day Molly had, as we always did after a session. I tried to tell Amanda specifics about how Molly communicated with me and played with peers appropriately, but she wasn't listening. Not only were her arms crossed the whole time, but she wouldn't make eye contact with me. Now, I don't remember the exact wording she interjected with at this point, but what I do remember is that expletives were used. They weren't necessarily directed at me, but they were **about** me. One specific thing she said stuck with me, though. She told me that her children don't get a "day off" of having a disability. She was correct, and this brought about immense guilt in me. Molly, Corey, and Ben **didn't** take a break from the difficulties they faced daily. The family also **didn't** take a break from caring for their children. I took a deep breath, handed her Molly's session note, and said goodbye, choosing not to engage. She was very angry, and I knew that nothing I would say would make it better at this point. Once the kids were gone, my best friend, a supervisor at the clinic, came out of her office after overhearing the end of Amanda's outburst. Although she said she didn't quite catch what was happening, she said she knew it didn't sound right. Naturally, this caused me to break down crying. We went into my boss's office, and I told her what happened. Both of them hugged me, which brings up a side lesson of the importance of finding safe and accepting workplaces. Work for—and with—people with similar professional values and morals as you do. I was so lucky to have the support of my boss and best friend during this situation, which was one of the hardest interactions I have had my entire time at the clinic, but also throughout my time with the company. Good employers are difficult to come by; hold on to them!

That same day, I had an evening session with another child, so I needed to shake it off and get back to being my best self. My next client deserved my best, and I wasn't sure I had it in me after this emotional day. Within a few hours of the interaction with Amanda, she emailed my boss and me. In the email, she expressed her apologies for her behavior. She shared that she had just been diagnosed with a very serious, potentially life-threatening illness. She gave more details about this illness, which brought me to tears, yet again. What an emotional rollercoaster that entire day was. I began thinking about the kids, questioning what would happen to them if something happened to her. Could Andrew and grandma take care of all of them? I seriously considered that I would take care of Molly if I had to, even at my very young age. This was an exaggeration of course, but I couldn't handle the thought of their family breaking apart in the absence of Amanda. I was completely devastated. I'm pretty sure I canceled my evening session that night.

To attempt to summarize what this experience taught me is difficult. I was completely devastated at the time, as I felt like the entire relationship we had been building for years at this point came crashing down. I was worried they would pull their children from services because I planned on taking a few days off around the holidays. My boss and best friend assured me that this was not my fault and that I did nothing wrong, but it was still very hard to accept. On top of that was the possibility of Amanda being terminally ill. I felt another level of guilt in being so upset about her behavior when there was an underlying reason like the one she had. Interestingly, down the road, we all found out that Amanda was misdiagnosed and would be fine after being given a new medication. We moved forward with small steps, as we rebuilt our trust and communication to continue to be Molly and her siblings' strongest advocates and teammates.

Flash forward a few months: I began working with Molly's siblings, Corey and Ben, too. At this point, I was working with Molly's family every day of the week. This meant a lot of parent conversations, notes home, debriefs at pick-up, and the like. This allowed me to get to know the family even more. It was important to me to take the time to continue to get to know all members of Molly's family because I felt a closeness to them that was difficult to put into words. It felt like we were truly on this journey together, at least from my point of view. I am proud of the early practitioner me, knowing, without much experience or training, that I needed to create a strong relationship and build trust with this family. I didn't use this approach just because I felt that it was the right thing to do. I simply did it because I cared so much about Molly and her family, and they were a huge part of my life. Despite the challenges practitioners may face when working with families, getting to know them and being a part of their

60   Love is Praxis

team to help their child succeed is absolutely one of the best parts of the job. It is what pushes you through the toughest days.

Spending the majority of my time with Molly and her family was fun and rewarding for the most part. When I started working with Corey and Ben, I began realizing something was starting to happen—something that I hadn't experienced yet. Although I was building confidence in my behavior analytic skill-building expertise, for some reason, Corey clearly didn't like me. I was trying to relate to him, play the games he liked, attempting to be fun and engaging, but unfortunately, nothing was working. I struggled with not being liked, which I imagine many people do. In spite of the fact that I felt like I learned the skills I needed to learn, worked hard, and had a positive attitude, why wasn't that enough for him to like me? It wasn't. As a practitioner, I learned that it is never as simple as being a good student and being good at your job when you're working closely with humans. Though I know and understand this, it hurts even now to think about not being liked by a child. Molly's parents recognized this was happening as well. Corey didn't want to come to our sessions and began engaging in escape behaviors to get out of attending. Because I had such a good relationship with the family, I felt comfortable talking to them about him not liking me. We worked together to build in fun, engaging, and reinforcing activities into the sessions as well as games that he might enjoy. We even bought brand new toys that he would like just for him! Unfortunately for all of us, this didn't seem to work either. Molly's parents told me that at school he **loved** his paraprofessional. She was his person, and no one else compared. At the time, this made me feel somewhat better. I thought, "Oh, I just can't compete with her. That's fine." In addition, Corey was going through puberty (as reported by the family) then, and the family felt that in all contexts of his life besides when with his paraprofessional, he was behaving in uncharacteristic ways. He was crying more, engaging in hitting, kicking, and spitting behaviors, and running away more frequently. Amanda and Andrew felt that puberty had a lot to do with these new behaviors. They reassured me that I shouldn't feel responsible somehow or that I was to blame. Now, reflecting on this conversation with Molly's parents, I feel guilty that I indirectly and subconsciously relied on them to make me feel better about not being liked by their son. That wasn't their job. They may have been right about what was going on with him during this time. However, they shouldn't have had to make me feel adequate at my job. While living in the guilt of this time in my early career, I am reminded of the complexity of the relationship with families in addition to the fact that I'm human and there is a deep vulnerability when working in a field supporting families. As much as I loved them and cherished my time with their children, I think they cared for me, too. I think they genuinely didn't want me to blame myself for Corey's behaviors or actions. In this relationship, we each gave, and we each took. There were ups and downs for all of us, not just Molly, her siblings, and her parents. As a practitioner, I learned that I can experience highs and lows too, just as the children I provide services to as well as their families. This doesn't negate the need for professionalism, tact, strength, and resilience one should have as a practitioner. However, I learned to **let** myself experience the feelings that come with working very closely with children with disabilities and their families and work through them. I am fortunate that, during this time, I was able to learn with **and** from Molly and her family.

Many ups and downs occurred throughout the years with Molly and her family. Molly and Corey made progress in their communication, daily living, and social skills. Each session was different; however, with each passing day, Molly and Corey grew in front of my eyes. Although some days were, of course, difficult, what I remember most fondly are the good days—days when we laughed and played and when they were able to be kids. The whole family grew so much over the years we spent together, and I grew as a practitioner, too.

COVID-19 happened and changed everything for the clinic, the families, and the kids for a long time. Everything was remote for a while, which was not as effective as we all had hoped. When the clinic was able to open again, the number of children we were able to see at once was very small but slowly increased. Also, during this time, I completed my supervision hours and passed my board exam. After many hours of studying, taking practice exams, and reading and re-reading textbooks, I was officially a Board-Certified Behavior Analyst (BCBA). I worked hard to be there, and I was so relieved! With my new title, I interviewed with the company I was already employed with for a BCBA position. Fortunately, I was hired, and within a few months, I began to build my caseload. Though I was empowered and excited to start my new position, one huge concern I had was no longer being able to work with Molly and her family. My boss, knowing how much they meant to me and the relationship I built with her family for years, was able to move caseloads around and told me that Molly would be on my caseload. I was ecstatic! In time,

Ben was also added to my caseload. This made perfect sense, based on the relationship I had with the family. This also made scheduling parent training sessions and phone calls that much simpler for the family, who already had to balance sports, therapies, school pick-ups, and other responsibilities. As with all of the years and experiences with Molly's family before, some days were successes, and some were quite challenging. However, we worked through the tough days together as a new team Molly, her family, their new Registered Behavior Technicians (RBT), and I.

The final chapter

The final chapter of this story is the most difficult one to retell. While this was the most challenging and upsetting period in my life, it was the one in which I learned the most as a practitioner. Unfortunately, not all lessons you will learn are due to positive experiences. Molly continued to thrive and grow, which was the most rewarding and heartwarming part of my time at the clinic. I often cried happy tears watching her dance around the clinic, sing, play with others, and express herself in creative and artistic ways. Corey, however, was going through difficult times. The behaviors he began exhibiting during sessions were extremely dangerous to himself, the staff, and other children. As his supervisor, I wasn't able to attend every session he had with his RBTs, but he required multiple staff members to keep him safe. At a certain point, I realized that not only was he unhappy but he wasn't learning from us anymore. I never wanted to do harm or upset a child, but I felt that, with him, we were no longer able to serve him in the best way anymore. I tried adapting all of his sessions, his treatment plans, and his behavior plans. We attempted to change the time and duration of his sessions. We tried switching staff. Nothing was working. He was unsafe and so unhappy. With the guidance and support of my boss and the clinical director, we decided that it was not productive and safe to serve him anymore. Nothing has ever been more heartbreaking for me than having to accept I was unable to help him. We felt that what he needed were services that were outside our scope of practice. We sat down with the family as a team to have this **very** difficult and upsetting conversation. I'm still surprised that I didn't break down until the meeting ended. Very understandably, the family did not take this news well. Though we were all in touch throughout these tough times, and his teachers were reporting very similar experiences at school, Amanda and Andrew were surprised and, what I would describe as, defeated. An air of defeat hung over us, including Amanda and Andrew. They seemed exhausted and broken down by everything they were going through. I knew they were struggling with this news and to find Corey the support he needed, and the fact that I couldn't help them made me feel inadequate as a practitioner. I felt incompetent. This was my entire job, to support my families, and I couldn't even do that. Even though I made the decision that I felt was the most ethical for everyone, and that we were unable to provide services that were beneficial to him, this was also not fair to them. We felt that he needed support in other ways, which we respectfully recommended to the family.

As quickly as the meeting with the parents started, it ended. They were terse with their responses and said some things out of frustration that, again, I understood. I wasn't in their shoes, but could empathize with their disappointment. Maybe they didn't know where to turn at this point if we couldn't serve them anymore, especially when he was experiencing the same struggles in school. I cannot imagine what this must have felt like, and I would never try to pretend that I could. I didn't know it at the time, but I would never see Molly again after this conversation. The family withdrew from services for all children, effective immediately, despite our intentions to implement a fading plan (recommended in cases like these) as well as provide the family with resources. I knew they wouldn't be my clients forever, but I dreamed of the day that Molly and her siblings were off on their own to school, playing sports, doing plays, with their proud mother posting on Facebook about her wonderful children. I believe that is happening, although I will never know, since the relationship was severed without any chances for revival. I wish so much that we could have maintained a professional relationship, but unfortunately, not every story has a perfectly happy or predictable ending. This was the hardest lesson for me to learn. If you care deeply, it is natural to grow close to families. This is human nature. However, at the end of the day, you are a practitioner serving and supporting a family, and at some point, that relationship will end, whether the child has immense success and no longer requires services, or if like Molly's brother, it fails to be an effective service. Some relationships carry on after this ending while others do not. However, no one can quite prepare you for the heartbreak of accepting that you aren't what a child needs, no matter how desperately you want to be.

Collaboration with families and other practitioners is a rewarding learning experience that requires all parties to listen to one another, to never lose sight of the fact that supporting the child is the central goal for everyone, and to respect the expertise of each individual, including the practitioner. I know that the way my relationship with Molly's family ended in the best interests of their child, but it did not happen the way we had hoped. I spent many days ruminating on what I could have done differently and better for them. I take responsibility for not being able to provide an appropriate environment for him to thrive, but I felt that I did the best I could for them at that time. I wish them the best always and will fondly remember my time with Molly and her family.

The beautiful parts

Having the privilege of knowing Molly and her family will have forever shaped me as a practitioner and person. Knowing Molly was the single most beautiful outcome of my early career. Not only did I develop as a practitioner alongside of Molly and her family, but the love I have for advocating for, working with, and supporting children and their families also grew to a level I would not have anticipated on that very first day so many years ago now, when I observed a very silly, spunky little Molly. If Molly ever finds herself reading this chapter, I hope that she recognizes all that she has accomplished and all that she has taught me. I hope that she and her family will read this chapter and remember the positive moments we all shared over the years with warmth. In addition, if they were to read this chapter, what I wish for more than anything else is for Molly and her family to discern how passionately I cared for them as well as feel the love I have for all of them to this day, regardless of the ups and downs we experienced. Thank you, Molly, Corey, Ben, Amanda, and Andrew.

Future practitioners: there are many lessons I hope you can take from this story. Overall, you should realize that relationships with families are deeply complex. There are highs and there are lows. You must take the time to know the families you work with, respect them, love them, and hear their wants, needs, concerns, and ideas. Sometimes, you will not be the right fit for a child, but at the end of the day, the child's growth and success need to be your central concern. If you no longer can help the family reach those goals, it is necessary that you be honest and try to find the appropriate party to support them. I don't think this conversation is ever easy, but sometimes it might be harder than most. The beautiful part of working with families of children with disabilities is the relationships you form and watching the children grow with the watering, sunlight, warmth, and love you provide alongside the family. At the same time, fostering a healthy and prosperous relationship means that, one day, it will most likely end, and the family will continue on their journey with their child to meet all of their needs in ways you are not able to be a part of. I implore you to enjoy the ride, do your best work for your families, and remember that things will get complicated along the way.

Reflective questions

1. Think about a time when you felt you could have handled a situation differently with a family. Did you do or say something that you would have done differently? What outcome would you have wanted from the situation? How would this have affected the family?

2. What are some ways to build rapport with families?

   a. What is the importance of getting to know a family?

3. How can you build in time for self-reflection into your practice?

4. Why is it important for you to remember the complicated nature of working with families of children with disabilities?

5
Too Much...
Not Enough

Julia Sledz

There is nothing in the world I hate more than making a phone call. The stress kicks in, and I start asking myself a million questions. What if I dial the wrong number? What if the person doesn't say hello? What if the line goes dead, like in one of those old murder mystery movies?

The last one is a stretch, but the phone call I was about to take had me terrified. See, after a full year of medical leave from college, my doctors finally gave me the approval to go back to classes. I could go if I lived at home and got accommodations from the disability office. What is the major problem with this plan? My disability isn't always viewed as a disability.

To make a long story short, I have had two major concussions in my lifetime. Technically, I suffer from post-concussion disorder, where the brain does not heal properly. The person then suffers from magnified concussion symptoms (Dwyer and Katz, 2018). Personally, my symptoms were constant nausea, dizziness, headaches, and vomiting. I also have a sensitivity to light and sound. My eyes were also affected, and I see in a completely different, exhausting way. My sleep is different as well, and I need to sleep about eight to ten hours on a given day. My body is completely exhausted by the end of the day, and often I am so physically exhausted that I stop being able to function. My anxiety skyrocketed. From these concussions, I developed migraines, and there are about three to seven days a month when I cannot function due to the pain I experience from them. During these migraines, I can lose control of my hands as they shake to the point I cannot function. I also developed an intolerance to gluten and dairy and cannot eat them as they trigger and magnify all my symptoms.

The phone call

The list above was the exact one I had made for the accommodation phone call. Concussions like mine are uncommon, and people have rarely heard of them. This made advocating for myself for the first time terrifying. The person would call me, listen to my speech, and then decide if I could have accommodations. Essentially, he also decided if I could continue going to class. The end of the speech was the letter my doctors had given me, listing my accommodations. They recommended extra absences for migraine days, a quiet testing space, and extra time for tests, as I still struggled to process things quickly. And at the end, all I could hear was him laughing. Laughing at me. At everything I had been through. At everything I was still going through. At everything I would still have to go through. He finally stopped laughing and said, "Sorry honey, that's not enough. Right now, you just sound like a college kid with a hangover."

He hung up right after that. And all I could hear in my head was "not enough". For the previous five years, all I had heard was how my concussions were too much. Too much to play sports again. Too much to go back to college classes. Too much to work. Too much to run. But now that wasn't enough.

Missing out

That call was four years ago. Today, I am in my last classes before getting my degree in special education. For all my success, I had a lot of struggles. Taking certain classes became too much, and I had to drop them. After classes, my body was so physically exhausted and I had so many migraines that I could not do extracurriculars. For most of my college career, I felt like I had had only half of the college experience. I got to experience in-person classes and get my degree, but I missed out on the other half of the college experience.

When I miss out on something I really wanted to attend, I often think back to that phone call. How could one person define who I was from one phone call? He could decide that my daily experience was not enough to warrant any help. This call makes me doubt myself often. I do not really know if I belong in the disability community. Often, I think that what that man said is true, that I do not go through nearly enough to be considered disabled. But when I start working next year, I will automatically receive disability services for my migraines. I will get extra days and time off so I can rest and go to appointments. These accommodations are like the ones this man laughed off so easily.

I have no idea if I am too much or not enough. I know the symptoms I still have from my concussions will stick with me. I also know that new symptoms will continue to pop up. This week, five years after my second concussion, my dentist told me I had damage to my teeth because of the various concussion symptoms. After all my experiences and classes in college, I have no idea whether I have a disability. What I have learned is how to advocate for myself and my students. My special education degree has taught me how assessments and judgments can harm people with disabilities. These assessments are often based on stereotypes and cause people like me to be misdiagnosed and ignored. I can use this knowledge to advocate not only for myself but also for my students. No longer will people like the man on the phone be able to define me. I define myself, and in the process, I have become an advocate for my students' needs.

Reflective questions

1. How can we view disability holistically, rather than jumping to conclusions based on disability by their name?
2. How can we support people who may not have common disabilities?
3. How can we advocate for people so that they receive the disability services they need?

6
Speaking Out: A Letter to the Reader

Karla Patricia Armendariz

Hi reader!

Allow me to introduce myself. My name is Karla Patricia Armendariz, and I am a first-generation college student and speech-language pathologist (SLP) who is pursuing her doctoral degree in communication sciences. I identify as a Mexican woman. In this chapter, I'll be sharing my own experiences. These experiences are focused on my years in grade school and my early professional years, specifically, when I worked as a paraprofessional at an elementary school in Florida. While I had personal encounters with children with disabilities before then, the impact of the professional years was so significant that it has helped shape how I approach interactions with families experiencing similar challenges.

However, before we delve into these stories, it is essential for me to express gratitude toward the families and mentors who taught me about advocacy. Thank you for also showing grace during moments where perfection eluded me. Your lessons remain etched deeply within my memory always. Last, reader, please bear in mind that all names mentioned here are pseudonyms and all ages have been changed out of respect for everyone's confidentiality.

Initial experiences

When I was in first grade in Canada, my encounters with classmates who had disabilities were influenced by the presence of paraprofessionals. Although my knowledge about the Canadian education system as a child was limited, I distinctly remember two students accompanied by a paraprofessional. This paraprofessional's role involved occasionally guiding the students in and out of the classroom. In my mind, I thought they were leaving for extra time in physical education, and I desperately yearned to join them. Importantly though, despite having different needs than mine, these students never felt like they stood out from the rest because having an aide around didn't seem unusual at all; they seamlessly blended into our learning environment.

Occasionally, the paraprofessional would also assist me, working patiently to ensure that I understood things as I was not proficient in English then. Reflecting on those early experiences, I realize they have profoundly influenced my approach to professional practice. I strongly believe in recognizing and celebrating everyone's unique qualities. Had the teacher kept disabled students apart from others or not permitted engagement with paraprofessionals, this contrast may have been even more prominent. In essence, my perception and early interactions with children with disabilities and professionals were shaped from an impressionable age.

As I progressed to third and fourth grade, a significant friendship blossomed with a classmate named Cathy, who also had the support of a paraprofessional. Cathy, who did not have expressive language at the time and who was occasionally overwhelmed to the point of tears, resonated with me. Amid classmates' curiosity regarding my conversations with my mom in Spanish, I connected with Cathy's experiences because the same students would also be curious about Cathy's way of communicating. What truly captivated me was her extraordinary skill at coloring.

I was seated next to her frequently and marveled at her meticulous approach when coloring. Cathy always ensured that every colored pencil stroke harmonized perfectly with the lines. To this day I try to emulate her coloring skills! Remarkably, it never dawned on me that Cathy carried an identity marker of a disability, and the teacher never underscored the fact that she had a dedicated aide. Cathy's presence, defined by her artistic abilities and the unassuming support of her paraprofessional, also left an enduring imprint on my perception of inclusivity. The classroom environment, characterized by a lack of emphasis on differences, cultivated a sense of belonging for everyone, no matter what labels we were assigned.

Looking back, those first experiences laid out a plan for identifying the innate value and abilities of people with disabilities. It was more than just obtaining knowledge; it also taught me empathy, demonstrating that true understanding stems from having shared encounters and mutual regard. This early introduction planted the beginnings of an all-encompassing outlook

76   Love is Praxis

that still affects how I perceive diversity today and shapes my involvement in society at large.

Speak up!

Skipping ahead to my first professional position, I began my journey as a paraprofessional working in a pre-kindergarten classroom in a very affluent area in Southern Florida. The classroom was known within the school for children labeled with "intensive needs". In my own experience, the label assigned to the children placed in the classroom seemed to impose certain biases on us as professionals even before we set foot inside. The designation of "intensive needs" created an immediate sense of expectation, as if I had to approach the classroom with heightened vigilance, anticipating that the students would be inherently "intense" and demand extra assistance. I hated the name. It was very deficit-based.

Entering this environment was like stepping into an alternate reality—an experience entirely unlike anything I had encountered before. The classroom itself featured distinct centers in each corner, adorned with visual schedules at every station. What struck me as particularly unique was the inclusion of a bathroom within the classroom, complete with a thorough stock of diapers and an extensive schedule detailing, down to the minutes, when each child should be guided to the toilet for potty training. The level of detail was intense.

The school took great pride in cultivating a diverse student community, with many students hailing from politically turbulent Latin American countries such as Venezuela and Colombia.

Interestingly, a significant portion of these students were not originally zoned for our elementary school. Instead, they were beneficiaries of the McKay Scholarship—a program aimed at improving accessibility for children with disabilities.

This scholarship allowed them to attend a public school outside their designated zone or choose a private school that better catered to their needs. The underlying premise was that the selected school would possess the necessary resources to offer tailored support for each child. Consequently, our school enrolled children with disabilities from families with considerable financial means, who were zoned for our school, as well as students from immigrant families who lacked the financial resources to enroll their child without the support of the McKay Scholarship.

As an immigrant, I personally witnessed the challenges my parents faced living in a country where virtually no one spoke their language at the time. At just four years old, there were moments when I had to step in as the translator for my parents when they tried to communicate with my teachers. Therefore, every interaction I had with a Latin American family with a child with a disability resonated deeply with me. I understood their experiences on a profound level.

However, I also recognized that, unlike my family's experience, these families faced an additional layer of complexity: learning to navigate the school system for their child with a disability. It added another dimension of difficulty to an already challenging situation.

In general, the school had a policy in place where paraprofessionals were permitted to interact with parents only during

78   Love is Praxis

pick-up and drop-off times despite spending the most time with the child. In addition, we were not allowed to participate in Individualized Education Program (IEP) meetings. I was granted what the school deemed an "extra privilege", which, in my view, felt more like tokenization. My role was limited to attending meetings requiring translation services. Being present in those meetings reminded me of translating for my own parents. This time, though, I was confined exclusively to being a messenger. I was a parrot relaying messages from other professionals who held higher authority. It was extremely frustrating for me to witness children being informed of reductions in certain services, seeing the parents' disappointment, and knowing the family had the right to contest it. I was unable to voice anything on their behalf.

Silence is not golden

"Hey, can you stay after school and help translate for me in Spanish?" asked Miss Jillian, as I was getting the students ready for dismissal. It was my second day, so I wanted to be a team player and agreed to stay behind and serve as a translator for a student named Baxter's teacher conference.

Before Baxter's mother, Elisa, arrived, Miss Jillian provided me with an overview of Baxter's background. Baxter, a three-year-old, was born to Guatemalan immigrants in their late forties who hadn't anticipated having more children after their first son (then 18 years old). Consequently, Baxter not only belonged to an immigrant family unfamiliar with the school's language but also found himself navigating a school system anew due to the considerable age gap with his older brother. Baxter's family lived

Speaking out   79

30 minutes away from the school. With the assistance of a social worker, the family managed to enroll him in the elementary school where I worked. Miss Jillian added that she suspected that Baxter might have autism since he didn't speak, yet she believed it wasn't her place to convey any suspicions to his parents.

Once Elisa arrived, Miss Jillian showed her various crafts Baxter made throughout the first half of the school year and commented on how Baxter gives the best hugs. This fifteen-minute conference ended too quickly for my liking; I wished we discussed more than just crafts and affection. I understood that telling the parent that she suspected autism was not within Miss Jillian's scope. However, she could have been more forthcoming, sharing the reality of Baxter's day-to-day life in the classroom. The lack of transparency left me incredibly disappointed, not only in the teacher but in **myself.** I felt so conflicted. My job was to translate Miss Jillian's statements, and yet I wanted to say so much more. I wanted to tell Baxter's mom that maybe having additional language support outside of school could be beneficial for him.

Reflecting on my first year, I still feel frustrated that pleasing us as professionals and avoiding conflict took precedence over standing up for the parents and forming an alliance. Can you imagine attending a dinner party where everyone is familiar with each other, leaving you with a feeling of being excluded from conversations? Even if this scenario hasn't happened to you before, it's not hard to grasp how unpleasant it would be. For many immigrant parents of children with disabilities—navigating a foreign country while placing their child in school, where language barriers abound—these situations can evoke similar emotions.

Despite the smiling faces of professionals within the educational system they encounter daily, communication remains incomplete at best.

As professionals, we often underestimate our influence and sometimes resort to gatekeeping. Reflecting on it, I don't believe a language barrier was the primary reason Baxter's parents were left uninformed about his challenges. I remained silent, initially due to my newcomer status, but in other instances, it was driven by the fear of potential consequences from the administration, particularly the head of the Special Education department in the school (Ms Lamp). I observed that Ms Lamp seemed more inclined to support teachers in cases where parents were less "high profile"—meaning those who caused fewer issues with the administration, resulting in less work for her and, subsequently, less work for the teacher. It seemed that Miss Jillian avoided addressing more significant issues to avoid potential backlash from her superiors. Overall, because of my lived experience in this world, I empathize with parents' disillusionment with the education system, particularly in Baxter's case. Our failure to communicate led to a loss of precious time for Baxter to receive the developmental support he needed.

Disability looks different for many families

Throughout Baxter's grade school years, I kept in touch with his family. He was diagnosed with autism right after the end of his preschool year, and this came as a shock to his family. Baxter's family believed that his difficulty in speaking, in general, was a result of his exposure to two languages, which they thought might be causing confusion for him. Elisa had initially blamed herself for her son's autism, believing it was somehow her fault. Elisa had mentioned how worried she was about what this diagnosis would mean for their child. In her home country and within her family, children with disabilities were often hidden away and deemed unable to survive independently. In the face of these challenges, many people, including myself, sought to reassure Elisa. We emphasized the uniqueness and potential of every individual, reiterating that we were all part of a shared journey.

Within my career as a paraprofessional, I gained an understanding that each family has their distinct perception of disability. This was exemplified in the case of Thomas, a seven-year-old boy with Down Syndrome whose parents viewed his diagnosis as a tremendous gift. They often spoke about how he brought immeasurable joy to their lives and shared his aspirations to become an actor when he grew up—which contrasted starkly with Elisa's perspective on Baxter's autism diagnosis.

To this day, I encounter multiple perspectives and attitudes relating to disability. These viewpoints are greatly shaped by the family's unique personal experiences and cultural backgrounds. The diversity within these accounts underscores the importance of promoting an inclusive atmosphere that acknowledges and honors each person's abilities. During my time supporting Baxter and Thomas, it was clear that developing awareness and comprehension surrounding their diverse (and sometimes hidden) capabilities played a vital role.

Broader advocacy

Being a part of Benny's story also influenced me greatly. Having relocated from Nicaragua, Benny came with his mother, Karina, an American-born Nicaraguan woman who returned to her home country after birth, as well as his father, Osvaldo, who didn't have legal status in the US. Karina and Osvaldo highly valued Spanish as a means to preserve their cultural heritage, and they were quite hesitant to learn and speak English.

Three years into Benny's education, he began to encounter significant challenges in the school setting. He had an autism diagnosis and was placed in a general education second-grade classroom with a monolingual English-speaking teacher. Benny was initially doing very well in this setting. However, from one day to the next, Benny was being removed from general education classrooms and placed in the autism support classroom due to his expressions of overwhelming sadness, accompanied by a stream of Spanish dialogue. While deciphering his words proved challenging, specific phrases, such as "Papa", echoed a deep sense of emotional distress.

Amid these difficulties, Benny's emotional regulation and ability to transition between tasks noticeably improved whenever he encountered me, as I spoke Spanish just like he did. The recognition and comfort derived from our shared interactions seemed to be a source of solace for him. His mother approached me during a morning pick-up with an urgent appeal to compose a letter to their family's lawyer regarding her husband's legal predicament after being stopped by Immigration and Customs Enforcement[12] (ICE). The request specified letters attesting to Benny's heavy reliance on paternal support given his diagnosis and routine-dependent lifestyle.

This unexpected twist shed light on the depth of Benny's familial challenges. It weighed heavily on my heart to realize that Benny was having a hard time at school because he was missing his father. Determined to aid his family, I drafted a letter to persuade their lawyer on Benny's behalf expressing his need for an unwavering and nourishing home atmosphere. The correspondence proved effective, culminating in the release of his father.

I will never forget the day I saw Benny walk up to school, joyfully skipping alongside his father. Tears of joy streamed down my face for the entire day. His story illuminated the intricate challenges families, educators, and students face in navigating the broader legal system.

Language was a bridge and a barrier

Upon arriving at the elementary school where I worked, Elias—a nine-year-old boy who was 5'6" and weighed approximately 180 lbs—appeared to be in an unhappy mood. He was lying on the ground in the front office area while yelling loudly. In attempts to assist him, his mother Maria called out "Vamos Eli!" as she tried picking him up by straddling across him. The intercom went off in the third-grade autism support classroom "Can Karla please come to the front office? We need assistance with a new student." **News to me that we were getting a new student in the class**, I thought.

As I was making my way to the front office, I ran into Elias who was walking happily holding his mom's hand on one side and the head of special education on the other. The department head quickly introduced everyone.

"Karla, this is Maria, Elias' mom; Maria, this is Karla, the paraprofessional in Elias' classroom." Before shaking Maria's hand, I went up to Elias and said,

"Hello Elias, I am Ms Karla", to which Elias responded, "Hello Elias, I am Ms Karla", and broadened his smile.

Maria then quickly asked me, "Hablas español?" ["Do you speak Spanish?"] and I responded "Si, mucho gusto." ["Yes, nice to meet you."]

"Ay que bueno que hay alguien que habla español. Nosotros nos cambiamos a esta ciudad porque yo, en verdad, no hablo mucho inglés." ["Oh, it's so good that there's someone who speaks Spanish. We moved to this city because, honestly, I don't speak much English."]

In this city, Maria was not an outsider but someone rather familiar. Several families emigrated from countries within Latin America with the majority coming from Venezuela and Colombia. At a young age, Elias received an autism diagnosis and continued to receive assistance in the form of a nanny until relocating here in the US. Upon arrival, he found himself attending class under the supervision of a special education teacher who did not speak Spanish. I could relate to Elias' situation as I had also personally experienced moving abroad to a place where my instructor did not share my native tongue.

Speaking the same language as Elias was extremely helpful in understanding his wants and needs as well as building connections with the family. I knew, however, that not being proficient in English could potentially be detrimental to Elias' parents advocating for him. Furthermore, after my experience with Baxter, I resolved not to repeat the same mistake of not saying anything and urged the classroom instructor to introduce Maria to another mother within the class who also hailed from Colombia, by the name of Isabella. This minor gesture produced tremendous benefits: Maria could better navigate through the school infrastructure and started to feel more integrated into her community.

Over the next few months, Maria and Isabella formed a powerful bond of support. Their shared cultural background not only helped them communicate effectively but also gave them the strength to navigate the intricate world of school together. Seeing their teamwork in action made me realize how small acts of connection can have a profound impact on building community within our school.

Two strong Latina matriarchs were transforming the school culture. With each passing day, Maria's involvement in school activities deepened, and she attended parent-teacher meetings with a newfound sense of self-assurance. Alongside Isabella, they advocated not only for Elias but also for many other non-English-speaking parents within the community. Their friendship blossomed into a community that supported each other. I felt as though there was a new air of inclusivity among many other families grappling with language barriers.

Introspective thoughts

During my time as a paraprofessional, I became aware of the systemic challenges that continue to marginalize vulnerable families. To tackle this issue effectively, I realized we need a more comprehensive approach. The interplay between school policies and political systems only added to the complexity of addressing these issues, which made it challenging for me to fully support the students and families in need. However, acknowledging these structural barriers gave me renewed determination to help break this cycle of marginalization, seeking new ways to enhance my role in helping vulnerable communities move forward with hope and positivity.

Hoping for a future

My journey of learning and advocacy has expanded into the academic realm, where my experiences have found validation among a select group of esteemed minds in the field. However, within the academic landscape, I've encountered harsh realities. Despite being invited based on the premise that my perspective as a bilingual speech therapist would be valued, I often find myself tokenized in meetings, with little acknowledgment of my intellect. Adding to the complexity, the voices of families of children with disabilities are predominantly white, which does not align with the reality I witness. The pervasive whiteness in this space not only necessitates my own advocacy for recognition but also compels me to advocate for those families who lack the platform to share their voices. Despite these challenges, my goal remains clear: to persist in learning and advocating for those whose voices deserve to be heard but aren't in the discourse.

To you, the reader, I hope that my experiences resonate with you and perhaps offer validation for you, as you navigate your own journey. For parents reading this, I want you to know that you have an advocate in your corner. My commitment to learning and supporting families is an ongoing endeavor, and I aspire to contribute to a more inclusive and empathetic educational landscape.

Reflective questions

1. How do you actively connect with others from diverse backgrounds in your current engagements?
2. Can you share instances where you may have encountered challenges in feeling heard or understood?
3. In your professional interactions, how do you foster a sense of cultural sensitivity and inclusivity when working with families from varying backgrounds?

7
"Listen"

Bianca Emma Stoutenburg

I can't understand him. I try to, at least. It's been years, but he still looks at me with his big almond-shaped eyes, waiting for me to finally know what he's saying. But he doesn't speak. And that's what frustrates me. The fact is that he just stares at me because he can't express what he wants through words.

I wouldn't trade my brother for the world, and having Down Syndrome and autism just contribute to the characteristics that make him unique. They don't understand him. They just baby him or make assumptions about his thoughts based on their own, thinking that will suffice. But I know it doesn't. I know he gives up most of the time when people don't listen to him. When they haven't been around him long enough to know that he needs ketchup placed in the bottom middle of the plate, chicken on the right side, and vegetables placed on the left side. Every time. But how would they know that if they didn't pay careful attention to him?

"Mmm." He grunts as he signals me to rewind his movie to a specific part.

"Mmmm." I rewound it too far and now he's mad at me.

90 Love is Praxis

"Mmmm." I fast-forwarded too much and now he's frustrated and crying.

I don't understand. I never understand. I don't want to be a bad sister at all. I just want to understand him, but it is so hard. I want to listen to him and how he feels but it just comes out in grunts. Maybe he's scared to talk to the family because he thinks that we'd make fun of him for the way that he sounds, but the truth is all of us are patiently waiting for the day he's comfortable enough to speak to us. That day will come, I'm sure of it. Some nights I pray to God that he will wake up one day and tell us what he had dreamed about, or what exactly he wants to eat for breakfast instead of my dad feeding him turkey bacon and hashbrowns every day.

Every birthday, I pray that this is the year that he will speak to me using verbal language.

I prayed for it on his fifth birthday.

I prayed for it on his eighth birthday.

I prayed for it on his eleventh birthday.

I pray for it on his thirteenth birthday.

But I know it is not in my control at all. It is hard to think outside of myself sometimes, especially because I think it affects me. But I don't know what it is like for my brother. The thoughts, ideas, beliefs, and opinions he has to give up on, in hopes of creating a compromise with the person that he is trying to communicate with. We use the alternative and augmentative communication (AAC) device to help him express his needs and wants, but a part of me hoped that he wouldn't have to talk through a tablet. So much can be lost through translation, such as if he so happened to change his mind in a split second on whether he wants cookies and cream ice cream or an ice cream sandwich. And I wouldn't know, because I was too busy looking into the freezer to notice that his facial expressions have changed, and he's signaling me to pay attention to him.

So many thoughts run through my mind about him, and I have created a sort of attachment style toward him. And because I love my brother deeply, I can't imagine him being in a world where he cannot stand up for himself.

When my mom and dad mentioned that they had placed him in a public school, my fears of bullying, harassment, and ridicule materialized out of thin air. My body froze and my face started heating up at the thought of not knowing how they would treat him in his new school. We were in the middle of nowhere, full of white folks, and he was a Black kid—with a disability. What type of support and advocate would he get in a place like this?

Of course, your own insecurities project onto your own beliefs and ideals, but I know how they treat children with disabilities. I'm not gullible. I have seen it with my own two eyes.

They grouped kids with different needs in one single class, with one single teacher to take care of all of the students. Students with autism, ADHD, Down Syndrome, or cerebral palsy were all expected to sit at one table, learning the same material. The class was housed in a building separate from the other students in my high school, and we never used to cross paths with them until lunchtime.

The administrators would have the students with disabilities all at one table, in the back of the cafeteria, isolating them from the rest of the students. All they could do was eat the food that the lunch lady had given them. They were expected to walk in and out of the cafeteria in a single file, treated like kindergarteners who could not stand uniformly because they constantly got distracted. However, I'm not surprised, because many people who don't understand the disability world treat individuals with disabilities like children who are not able to take care of themselves even the slightest bit. This is infantilizing, and people are beginning to recognize how harmful this behavior is toward people with disabilities, partly because people are speaking up (Safta-Zecheria, 2018). But what about people who, for whatever reason, cannot speak up for themselves?

The worst memory of high school had made its home comfortably in my mind for years. I try to escape it because of my disbelief, but it is impossible because I have seen it with my own two eyes. Spanish class was monotonous anyway, but that day was different. We had all sat doing our work when the sound of a knock filled the room. The class was already quiet because we were occupied with our studies, but the room fell quieter as I saw a girl with autism walking into the room with a trash bag.

Although the special education teacher stood a reasonable distance away from the student, she still invaded her space with her watchful eyes, monitoring the girl closely. The special education teacher apologized for disrupting the class and announced that they were there to complete one responsibility: to pick up the trash around the school. The other students in the special education class stood closely behind as well, holding trash bags, gloves, and a big bin in which they put the garbage. I had never felt so much pity and disgust in my life, resenting the administrators for allowing this type of behavior. The only students that I knew of who were to pick up trash from the school were the delinquents: these were students who disobeyed the code of conduct and picking up trash around the school served as their punishment. But why are we punishing young students with disabilities?

"That's **crazy**." Jazmin responded when I told her about the situation.

"They had made them pick up the trash girl, on a regular day. What was the purpose of treating them like that? They're literally treating them less than us, for no reason."

"Hmm. That is **wild**."

But I expected more from her. I expected the same amount of discontent that resided within myself and some solution to make this problem go away. But it wasn't much of an issue for her because it didn't affect her. Why would it? She didn't know how much protection children with disabilities needed. Or more so, she didn't care. For her, it didn't make the world stop. It didn't make her feel stressed. It didn't make her upset. It had nothing to do with her—it wasn't her problem. And so, I sat there by myself, with no plan of action. Just a 17-year-old girl who had faced the harsh reality of this cruel world.

…

"Retarded."

The word burns my chest every time I hear it. Of course, before my brother Isaiah came into this world I had thought the word was funny, a casual term to use when someone was being stupid. But now, my body tightens and my eyes become heavy. Hearing people use the word hurts me now, putting me in a position where I am to stand up for my brother as if I am standing up for myself. This is a word we have to stop using casually (Pulrang, 2021). Sometimes it's hard because it's my close friends. Sometimes it's a stranger that I have just met. Sometimes it's my own teacher.

I remember I was in the car of a boy that I really liked from my campus. It was late at night, and he said he wanted to pick me up to get something to eat. The windows were rolled down, with the air blowing my hair and seeping through my lungs, as he sped through the roads of State College going 70 mph. My adrenaline was high and my emotions were all over the place, feeling so overstimulated to the point where I clung to my seat, unable to do anything but control my breathing. He gave me this feeling constantly, this feeling of being on top of the world. Especially when he sped through the streets of this weird town.

We sat in the parking lot of the YMCA talking about the most random events that have happened in our lives and strange facts that would have been weird to tell other people. It felt so intimate.

"So, he really slipped on the floor after there was a whole sign that said caution?" I said as I laughed.

"Yeah, I honestly don't understand why he did that," he said

"That is so stupid."

"Yeah, that man is retarded[13]."

And there it was. That word. The one word I did not want him to say. The one word that hurts my chest every time that I hear it. The one word that puts me in a position where I have to choose him or my brother.

The car felt silent and the energy shifted. He saw how my face changed and the light in my eyes had died once he said that word, switching from a face of glee to a face of despair.

"I'm sorry Bianca, I shouldn't have said that..."

He knew. He knew how much it hurt me when he said that. He knew that I had a brother with Down Syndrome, and he knew how much I cared about my brother. It wasn't a situation of ignorance anymore; it was his choice of words. He chose to use that verbiage. And so, I looked at him with disappointed eyes, knowing that I couldn't continue seeing him as this soft, empathetic, and inclusive guy that I have always wanted him to be, but rather someone who could possibly make fun of individuals with disabilities behind my back.

My brother was at home at the time, probably watching videos on his iPad of Siberian Huskies running around, oblivious to the fact that the outside world is so cruel to him. There are people in this world who still use these words that were once used to degrade people with disabilities, including him. But Isaiah doesn't understand how dark the world is. His pure heart shines through each and every day, unaware of the way people try to "dumb him down". He doesn't know yet. But I do. I understand. So, I grabbed my items that lay comfortably in the cup compartment, put on my coat, and opened the car door, revealing the silent dark night in front of me.

"Where are you going?" He asked.

"I'm walking home."

"Why? Because I just said one word?"

"See, that's the problem you don't understand. It's offensive to me because it's offensive to my brother. And you knew that. Goodnight."

And there I was, walking down the street by myself, leaving the boy that I thought I once liked. But I don't care about him more than I care about Isaiah, and I would stick up for my brother no matter what.

I titled this essay "Listen" to encourage teachers, school personnel, community members—and, most importantly, our friends and family—to listen to children who don't have verbal language expression, to see them as human beings and not just their label. I can still recall the many things I have witnessed while learning about disability history in my studies and in my everyday encounters with people. They have very deficit and dehumanizing views; they use words that are harmful and disrespectful, and are infantilizing in their behaviors. Listen to them beyond the narrow ways you think they should express themselves. Listen also to those of us who are standing up for people who are not able to advocate for themselves in the same ways. Language is power, but it isn't the only power. Love is so much greater than the sum of all of our talents and gifts. And Isaiah, my brother, is love.

Reflective questions

1. What are some of the tensions you might feel when you want to understand someone who communicates differently? How does this author acknowledge and manage her own frustrations when her wants and goals don't match her brother's presentation?

2. How have students with disabilities in your school been treated? What are the expectations of them, and what does this communicate to the rest of their peers?

3. Why do you think it is important for people in the person's environments to learn how to listen? What is it they need to listen to?

4. What do you think the author means by "language is power, but it isn't the only power"? What is she stating about her brother? What can teachers take away from this?

8

How Does It Feel to Be a Woman with a Disability in a Developing Country?

Nayma Sultana Mim

> My grandmother never loved me because of my physical disability. She used to yell at me when I was a child and keep ranting over how I would be a burden to the family because no one will ever marry me. — Maria (pseudonym), a physically disabled woman

As a female practitioner in a developing country, I have come across persons with disabilities (PWDs) who have experienced a plethora of challenges throughout their lives in order to meet even the most basic necessities. Even though we live in a "modern society", a good number of people in developing countries still hold many myths and superstitions that result in a negative perspective toward disability. Besides, the social structure limits the independent living scope of the PWDs, which eventually results in engendering a sense of burden in society. It always bothered me to think about the structural hierarchies that restrict groups of people who are deemed "atypical", though this social structure has been established for all the people living in a society. However, society was not supposed to be structured for only one type of people considered "common" or "general" when there are hundreds of diversities among the human population. I have always been troubled by terms such as "common" or "general", as I have never understood why individuals with disabilities, who are also a part of our diverse society, are not included in the "common" or "general" population. Even now, in this twenty-first century, we as a society have not been able to stop practicing ableism.

Getting the opportunity to pursue my doctoral study in the US has created a handful of opportunities for me to learn about the lifestyles of PWDs in a first-world country. I am learning about the services received by both PWDs—starting from when they were newborns until they reach adulthood—and their families. Although the US-based practitioners are not satisfied with the services provided to PWDs and their families, it is overwhelming to learn about the current level of services such people receive here when compared to those living in developing countries. I acknowledge the huge difference between developed countries and developing ones in terms of economic status, but what I think is the most significant difference is the perspective on disability.

Disability perceptions: a global perspective

Being a PWD comes with all its own difficulties for the person in a developing country, and the experiences of the PWD get worse when another identity intersects with the disability identity, such as the gender identity of being a woman. Though gender discrimination sounds like a topic from ancient eras in developed countries, women living in developing countries are still struggling with establishing their rights. To this day, people pray for women to be pregnant with a boy rather than a girl. Gender roles are still restricting women from achieving their rights, and no matter how much education is acquired by women, they are still nurtured by society, either directly or indirectly, to become supporters of men rather than to become independent individuals in the community (Alur, 2021). In this circumstance, when disability intersects with the gender identity of women, their journey becomes more unique and challenging in the context of developing countries (Quinn *et al.*, 2019). The most depressing aspect of this is that the majority of the women start experiencing difficulties at home. It can be their parents, grandparents, or even siblings who hold a negative perspective toward these women with disabilities. Their gender identity shapes the experience of their disability identity, and vice versa. This negative attitude of the family members is related to various aspects, such as religious misconceptions, social norms, the unstable future of the family member with a disability, the lack of possibility to become a supporter for the family, and the feeling of creating difficulties for the family to live their typical social life. Besides, especially for women with disabilities, family members become conscious of how society sees and treats women with disabilities. A lot of discussion has been done in terms of the misconceptions of people that relate to their religious beliefs and the instability of economic benefits for women with disabilities. However, little has been discussed about the possible difficulties women with disabilities have to experience due to the lifestyle—or, in a broader sense, the social structure—in developing countries (Rao, 2024).

In developing countries, the lifestyle of the citizens is quite different and traditional when compared to those of developed countries. Due to the social structure, not the child, it takes a lot of patience, time, and money to take care of children with disabilities in a traditional society. Providing medical services, education, transition services, and employment opportunities to rehabilitation facilities in adulthood brings a lot of struggles for family members. As these services are not easily accessible, it becomes a huge responsibility for the family to nurture PWDs in developing countries without economic solvency. Besides, the social practice of raising daughters and then just marrying them off to another family brings the thought that spending money and time on women with disabilities will be of no use in the future as they are not likely to be married off, or, in a more dehumanizing word, they are not likely to be of any "use". This very utilitarian perspective is perhaps the most common reason behind the negative perspective among family members, who are already enduring the economic and social challenges in a developing country. Fighting for every single service and right sometimes makes it tough for family members to support their more vulnerable members. But how long and how much? Very few families out there can show up and support women with disabilities to fight against the social structures that create barriers to achieving the services they need.

The mothers who carry us forward

> My mother requested the school authority to keep my exam hall on the first floor as she thought that she wouldn't be able to carry me to the fifth floor. However, they did not keep the request and set my seat on the fifth floor. I remember how my mother then carried me using the stairs while no one came to help her. —Shilpi (pseudonym), a physically disabled woman

Even with the limited resources and services, there are a few women with disabilities in developing countries who are overcoming these barriers, receiving a formal education, involving themselves in income-generating activities, and serving their communities with the support of their loved ones. This does not mean that the families of these women are rich and that they do not have to continue dealing with economic and social challenges. Rather, this is the love of the mothers, their perspective on disability, and the willpower to support the vulnerable member in achieving their goals. It also proves how capable these women with disabilities are that, with minimum resources and support from their families, they try to overcome the challenges and fight back. I believe that this is the love of their close ones that provides them the strength to fight against the odds of our societies. It can be stated with assurance that if these people could receive support and services similar to those in developed countries from the community, then they would have participated in the development of their family, community, nation, and even the world to make it a better place.

A crying need for a disability-friendly tertiary[14] education system

Until recently, it was difficult for children with disabilities to attend any type of educational institution in developing countries. Before making it compulsory for all schools to admit children with disabilities, school authorities should consider the principles used to deny the admission of children with disabilities. The authorities not only admitted children but also demotivated those parents who wished to educate them. Things were even more challenging for girls with disabilities, as parents never considered educating girl children in the first place. In addition, to ensure their daughters' safety and avoid any unwanted situations, as the rate of rape cases among girls with disabilities was quite high, parents preferred to keep their daughters with disabilities at home in most cases.

Things have changed a great deal, and nowadays more children with disabilities, especially girls, are going to educational institutions. However, the services these students receive are not up to the mark, as there are no structured educational services for students with disabilities in developing countries. Overcoming these systemic challenges, some of the girls with disabilities persist and successfully complete school and college. However, only physically, visually, and hearing-impaired women can be seen at the tertiary level. Though these women overcame difficulties during their school and college days, things became very challenging for them at the tertiary level. Due to their daughters' age, parents of young girls worry about their marriage and voice their concerns in this regard to their children, which in turn greatly affects the mental health of women with disabilities. In many societies, even those women who don't have any disabilities go through tremendous social pressure of marriage during their tertiary education. In most cases, women with disabilities have to stay in university hostels, where they hardly receive their need-based services. They have to depend on other students to take them to classes and perform basic activities. A lot of women with disabilities experience depression because they have fewer friends and social systems, and they have to deal with a lot of challenges alone. Due to the mainstream system at the tertiary level, students with disabilities often face unfair situations; even after they successfully graduate after overcoming these challenges, they have to fight hard to find a job.

> I had moments when I was so anxious about managing a writer for my exam that I considered suicide to be my finest course of action. I wondered what would have happened if I fell off the third-floor balcony. —Mina (pseudonym), a visually impaired woman

Transition hopes

Career opportunities have become so scarce for the common people in developing countries that individuals with even a master's degree are unemployed, unable to get even low-paid jobs. However, there are a few governmental and nongovernmental organizations that create opportunities for PWDs to promote economic development. Sometimes, companies decide not to appoint PWDs because of the structural barriers in our society that can restrict the person's ability to work efficiently or be perceived as a beneficial employee for the organization. Without a disability-friendly transportation system, appropriate building infrastructure, and accessible devices, it becomes challenging for PWDs to productively contribute to the organization.

Things are more difficult for women with disabilities because none of these systems is women-friendly. Thus the problem women with disabilities face is twofold (Quinn *et al.*, 2016). Neither do they have the opportunity to work in most organizations, nor is the work environment in these places suited for PWDs to perform productively. However, some women with disabilities do find job opportunities through networking or a special recruitment process that is offered by the organizations as a charity in some cases. However, in most cases, job profiles do not match their academic qualifications.

> I have a master's degree in education, but now I am working in a garment factory, collecting objections from the employees. Sometimes, I sit alone all day and do nothing. All my degrees are of no use to me now. What will I do with my degrees now? —Pushpa (pseudonym), a visually impaired woman

Women with disabilities who get the opportunity to work in their desired positions often work twice as hard as their male colleagues, yet in many cases, they do not receive any increments at the end of the year. In addition, women with disabilities experience severe depression because of the mistreatment from their colleagues. In most cases, they remain silent about these experiences because of their increased vulnerability. They often choose not to raise their voice against the bias out of fear of losing their job and becoming a burden to their families. Their despair is exacerbated by the fact that they worry about losing their families as most of them never get the opportunity to get married and start their own.

Apart from family, educational institutions, and the workplace, we all live in a community where hope to feel a sense of belonging. A peaceful and cooperative community can be helpful for individuals to maintain a healthy lifestyle. Although there used to be a strong bond among neighbors that lasted until the late twentieth century, nowadays, people are not as connected due to the growth and fast pace of city life. Even in rural areas, people have started leading independent lives and communicating less with their neighbors. It has become very difficult even for individuals without disabilities to remain mentally healthy in this type of modern society, and PWDs living in urban areas are more likely to have worse mental health and lifestyle (Roy *et al.*, 2023; Shohel *et al.*, 2022). I have seen many cases where people choose not to disclose to their community the fact that they have children with disabilities at home just to avoid their stares and the stigma that follows. However, PWDs sometimes encounter people from the community when they go to school, college, or university. They also meet with other people at social events hosted by different organizations. Even in the workplace, people may find a lot of people with whom they can socialize at some point in their lives. It should be noted that this is not the case for everyone, and I have seen a lot of people spend their lives without any sort of socializing; this is especially true for women with disabilities who experience this challenge more than their male counterparts. A woman with visual impairment, for example, once stated that she had to stay vigilant of the fact that she could not fall while walking or risk bumping into other male members on the road because it would be more than shameful for her. Thus, she preferred to stay at home without socializing or communicating with other people in society, which led to her becoming more depressed with every passing day. Appropriate steps should be taken for women with disabilities by providing mental health support. More urgently, however, people need to change their perspective toward disability as well as support PWDs in the long run.

The long road ahead

Individuals with disabilities, especially women with disabilities with whom I have met and worked in my entire academic and professional career, have inspired me to fight against the difficulties of everyday life and work for a more just and equitable world where people with diverse abilities will find their need-based services. I hope for an education system where a student with learning disabilities will not be labeled as "bad". I also dream of a world where a woman with any physical disability does not have to think twice about transportation before leaving her home in the morning for work. And to establish this fair world, we have to embrace the praxis of love for diversity, replace deficit-based approach, and stop practicing ableism while forming policies and legislation.

In this chapter, I have tried to highlight the areas that are not well discussed in the current literature for women with disabilities living in developing countries. The aim of this chapter was to illustrate the experiences of the people who are trying to overcome the structural limitations of our societies, while also taking part in conquering the world. While it may be challenging for developing nations to offer support systems that are comparable to those in developed countries, women with disabilities from developing countries can still exercise their rights with a shift in perspective toward PWDs and, most critically, toward women with disabilities. With this change, the establishment of policies and infrastructure will pave the way for the PWDs to receive the services they deserve, with a positive outcome for families who can then focus their energy and lend support to their loved ones.

Reflective questions

1. In this twenty-first century, how can you raise awareness of disability around the world using love as a tool?
2. What initiatives should be taken to mitigate the challenges experienced by women with disabilities in developing countries?
3. What are the accommodations and supports (e.g. disability, physical health, mental health, library access, nutrition, etc.) women with disabilities receive at the tertiary education level in developed countries, and how can these accommodations be localized in developing countries?

9
Finding Myself through Autism

Ava Herr

For as far as my memory takes me, I have been surrounded by disability. I can confidently say that I didn't actively pursue a life that was so involved with the disability community, but that's how it turned out. I can't say I'm upset about it, but I can say that it has become a funny coincidence over time. Whenever I meet a new person, one of my first thoughts is if the person may be neurodivergent in some way. I have built an incidental rapport of being friends with, dating, and just generally being around people with some experience of disability. But as I reflect, there was a short period of time when I wasn't so involved in the disability community.

For the first three years of my life, I was the only child to my mother and birth father. My mother had given birth to me the week of her high school graduation, effectively letting me steal the show. I remember there being a really miserable picture of my mother in her hospital bed with her cap and gown, mostly because my grandma still wanted her to wear it. I have only heard rumors of this picture since my mother has buried its existence from the time I could form memories.

Because of my mothers teen pregnancy, we lived with my grandparents for the better part of eight years. Its been a very long time since I have stepped foot in that house since my grandparents have since moved, but I could draw a complete blueprint, down to the very spot where my grandfather kept his newspapers. I usually like to tell people that I was raised by my mother and grandmother since they were my primary caregivers. My grandfather typically worked during the days that I was awake, which left me to either stay at the house with my grandmother or go along with her to the nursing home where she worked. My mother worked a typical nine-to-five job, so I really spent time with her only on weekends and evenings. My birth father, on the other hand, really couldn't care less about what I was up to. I can't recall us ever doing anything together, but I do remember he was employed for the majority of the time when I was quite young.

Almost a month before my third birthday, however, my sister would enter the picture. I remember my mom bringing my sister home for the first time. I was obsessed with her as soon as she came through that front door. I adored her chubby cheeks, dark brown eyes, and her full head of long dark hair. Ever since my sister entered our world, I felt this almost natural protectiveness toward her, feeling as if *I* finally had a role in life. My mother can greatly attest to my sick adoration of my sister. There were multiple occasions where I would be found scaling the sides of her crib, just so I could snuggle with her in the middle of the night. Even if it wasn't nighttime, it was almost like we were attached at the hip, so much so that it was almost impossible for anyone to not be able to find me, as I was always right next to my sister. I even began having a strange compulsion where I would grip her hair, shove my face onto her scalp, and aggressively sniff while my body would shake, almost like a rapid shiver. At the time, I wasn't sure why I felt the need to attack my sister so randomly, but I realize now it was from that common sought-out smell of a baby. I continue to have this impulse with smells, such as the smell of my pets. No one has ever enjoyed it, especially not my sister, since I can vividly remember regularly getting scolded by my mother who would say, "Stop sniffing your sister!"

As we both grew older, I learned more about how my sister was different from me. I remember that I loved to go out to places like the park, but those periods of time would sometimes be cut short. We couldn't go to certain places for long periods of time because there was too much happening—too much sensory input for my sister. I remember there being times when I would be playing at the playground with a group of friends I had gathered together when suddenly my mom would yell to me that it was time to go. We had barely even been there! I had just started to play with these new friends! Of course, I would listen, but it was never because I wanted to but simply because I wanted to be able to come back later.

Restaurants were the same deal. I loved to go out to new places, especially to try out different cuisines, but we usually just bought take-out or fast food. On the rare occasions that we would sit down at a restaurant, my mom would spend more time consoling my sister than actually eating her own food. I never understood why, thinking that maybe siblings did strange things like this anyway.

I also remember that my sister would wake up at random times in the night and would just scream for what felt like forever. When we both got a little bit older, we shared a room together. I had gotten used to my little sister becoming randomly inconsolable, bringing our tired mother in to sit with her for some time. It almost became a routine; my sister would start screaming, I would try to console her, my mom would come in and try her best, and then my sister would randomly just relax. I began having nightmares when I was quite young, so I assumed she just kept having them too.

From my little brain, I had also started to perceive my sister as being really rude. Until I was about six years old, my sister spoke very little, if anything at all. By this period, I had entered HeadStart, and soon I started to realize how abnormal it was that my sister wouldn't talk to anyone, even if it was an adult. It was about the time I was about to start pre-school when things began to change.

We started to go to places that I wasn't familiar with. In particular, I remember there being a large building with a lot of doors leading to smaller rooms. The small rooms looked similar to my HeadStart class, but there were a lot more adults in the room.

We would also visit doctor's offices a lot more often, or stay there for a longer period of time. Here, the questions never ended, making me tired and causing more frustration for my sister as this meant restricted time away from desirable activities. All I really remember from those appointments was the doctors repeatedly asking my mom whether Emma was still allergic to a particular

Finding myself through autism   115

food coloring. All the while, Emma continued to increase her fussing as the appointments became longer and longer.

Emma wouldn't be able to use speech until I was about five years old, which put her age at three. Long, arduous efforts were definitely made to get my sister access to services, but all that I saw was a stranger who came over with a bag of toys to my grandparents' house. She would come into our house, wearing clothes like a teacher, and would sit on the floor criss cross applesauce next to my sister. She always had this giant gray Fisher Price Little People castle, which she would set up between my sister and herself. As soon as that castle was assembled, my mom would usually come around to tell me I needed to busy myself in my room until the stranger was gone. I believe there was only one or two times I got to stay and play with my sister and the castle. It felt like such a privilege to play with such an awesome toy.

Despite being told to play in my room, I would continue to eavesdrop as the stranger would encourage my sister to use her speech. That castle did wonders! There must have been some magic inside of it… I never heard Emma talk so much before! The stranger would ask her to make an animal sound, name the animal, or tell the characters what to do; words would just slip out with no effort at all.

There was another group of strangers that started to visit our home around this time—this was when I started to attend HeadStart at what would later become my elementary school. This group would wear just simple jeans and T-shirts, usually with a Nittany Lion on it. They would sit on my grandmother's couch, ask my mother questions, then try to play with my sister just like the other stranger would. I really only knew as much about this process because I would sometimes be asked to come out and answer questions about how my sister interacted with me. I continued to eavesdrop while pretending to occupy myself with a toy in my room. The interaction between my mother and this group of strangers would always end with everyone thanking one another; they would then make my mother sign a paper and hand her money afterward.

While all of these strangers would visit my house, I started to take the short yellow bus to my HeadStart in the morning. I would wear my large backpack, buckle up in my seat, and would head over to my classroom. I vividly remember feeling left behind in class, mostly because I wasn't able to read like my peers. I wouldn't be able to read until the summer before kindergarten, but until then, I memorized certain books so that my teachers thought I was able to read. I became really good at pretending to point at each word of Humpty Dumpty as I "read". One of my favorite places to go in my HeadStart room was this wooden high-rise, where there was a small ladder that led to a wooden platform loaded with various pillows and blankets. If anyone went looking for me, they were sure to find me nestled in a mountain of fabric. I was one for the dramatics up in that high-rise, always requesting that my lunch tray be handed up to me instead of me climbing down to eat with the others. I became such a dramatic young person that one of my teachers, Miss P, even started to call me Eva Longoria, a popular actor from the television show, *Desperate Housewives*.

When I eventually made the transition to kindergarten, I probably had the easiest time. Most children on my long yellow bus cried as if their parents were being ripped away from them, never to be seen again. I was truly upset only because the bus didn't have seatbelts. I loved to be at school since there were always new things to do and learn. One of the skills I was happy to continue and develop in this setting was my story reading.

As I entered kindergarten, I became very confident in my ability to read. My mom made sure we frequently went over to the local library, whether it was to play in the children's area or to pick out a new bedtime story. I wanted to show my old teachers what I had learned during the time I was gone, so I began visiting my old HeadStart room down the hall from my kindergarten room. It started as a lousy excuse to see my sister, since she had started HeadStart right when I had left, but it eventually became more than that. Miss P recommended that I read circle time books to Emma's class, which I happily obliged. Emma's classmates always looked forward to when I would come down during my lunch period to read, and I always looked forward to getting to spend more time with my sister.

The kids from her HeadStart classroom started to know me so well by the end of kindergarten that, when her class started kindergarten, they would ask me to push them on the swings on the playground. As a second grader, it became my job to push the younger kids on the swings. We even started a game where we could see how many kids I could help push on the swing set at a time.

Within my elementary school building, it was almost seen as a sort of graduation when you were given the opportunity to go to the second floor for classes. HeadStart through second grade all had classrooms on the first floor, but as soon as you started third grade, you were allowed to use the stairs to get to class! I felt like I was one with the older kids now.

Along with being on the second floor of my elementary school, the students in grades three through six got recess after the younger grades, with a very small amount of overlap. Usually, the younger kids would be on the playground by the time we headed outside, allowing us to play with them for around ten minutes before the younger grades began to line up and head back inside. I was more than thrilled to use those ten minutes to play with my sister, since she would have been in about first grade at this time.

I had known that Emma had other interests when playing outside, as she usually kept to herself in the small, wooded areas lined with picnic tables. She enjoyed making piles of wood chips below her feet, and often she tried to see how tall a pile she could create. As my grade was allowed to go outside right when Emma was finishing her magnificent mountain, I went over and helped pile more pieces on. Her teacher blew the whistle shortly after, alerting the younger students to begin lining up on the blacktop. My sister and I then worked together to put the wood chips back where they were before she skipped back over to her classmates, picking at smaller pieces left on her pant cuffs. I tried my best to ensure that the area was restored to how it originally appeared, eventually jogging over to the sidewalk to wave goodbye to my sister as she headed back into the building.

However, I was interrupted by one of my classmates. He wasn't one of my friends from class, but I thought it was important to be friendly to others too. He remarked to me that my sister was "weird" and how "she didn't play with the other kids", even going so far as to ask, "What's wrong with her?"

I had seen in shows before, like the cartoon *Tom and Jerry*, how characters' faces would swell up and turn into a bright red color, with steam rushing out from their ears, whenever they were angry. I didn't think an actual person could feel that way, but I was so overcome with emotion at that moment that I felt like my facial expression could have been taken straight out of that show. My fists tightened into balls, and all I could think about was landing a fist right into that smirking face, looking up at me with not a clue of my intentions. **How could someone say such cruel things about a person? He doesn't even know the first thing about my sister! Who cares that she does things differently? She enjoys the time she spends with herself and that's all that matters!** As my fists shook with the anticipation of leaving a mark right on his face, I decided to unclench them. My mother wouldn't appreciate having to pick me up from the principal's office afterwards, or even having to leave work early because I couldn't control myself. At that moment, I was hit with the horrible reality that people didn't have the same respect that I did when it came to allowing others to do what made them happy. If an action was dissimilar to their own, it was the strangest thing they had ever seen. They couldn't conceive that another person could simply be different from them.

My mom wasn't happy with my actions after that incident anyway since I chose to scream in his face and run off crying. One thing that brings me consolation is that at least she didn't have to hear about it from a teacher. Since then, however, a seed was planted: Emma was now **weird.**

Even after that experience, I carried on as any young child would. I continued to play with my group of friends at recess, ensuring that I ignored the particular student who had inevitably changed my perception of my sister. I began distancing myself from her, not because I was embarrassed about her differences, but because I didn't want my peers to feel the urge to address the said differences.

Later on in my third-grade year, I started to wander around with my friend groups. Not by choice this time, but because we were not allowed to play the game we had made up on the playground anymore. A friend and I had created a sort of tag-like game, which we called "The Walking Dead". One person would start as a zombie while the rest of the players were survivors. The zombies would run around and tag as many people as possible, turning them into zombies until there were no survivors left. A boy in my class, whose mother had grown close with my mom, gravely misinterpreted the rules of the game! Instead of tagging people, he started to physically bite people and leave marks. Later on, I came to know that this individual had what was then described as Asperger's Syndrome[15], which was why he may have reacted the way he did. He was notorious for having a short fuse and quite explosive reactions, especially to bees. I was upset at him, not because of his disability, but because we weren't allowed to play the game I had created anymore.

After our tag-like game was banned, I started to find other groups of individuals to hang out with. Our game was a smash

Finding myself through autism   121

hit, so many of the people who were used to playing with us had dispersed after the game was banned. On the other side of the playground, past the blacktop and the sidewalk leading to the building, there was a grassy area with trees and an outdoor theater. There were always a few students sitting on the grass in this area, playing similarly to my sister. One child would flutter his arms and spin in circles, squinting up through the leaves high up on the trees above. And just like how our teachers would watch us on the playground during our recess time, there was a smaller group of adults that stood together, facing the separate grassy area. There was no rule saying we couldn't go over to this part outside the school, and hence, I decided to venture past the playground where my classmates were.

I had noticed this group of kids previously but felt like there was some unspoken rule that we were not allowed to go over to them. They always came outside with the younger kids, leaving just before my class would. I didn't know which classroom they had come from, but I assumed it was a class similar to my own. There was one young boy, around my age, adorned with freckles on his face. He was by himself but seemed to enjoy his own company, just as my sister would. I walked over to him and asked if I could play with him, to which he was absolutely elated. I think that was the first time I had seen someone's eyes shine like that before. From then on, instead of immediately turning to the left outside the school doors, I would stray away from my classmates to look for my new friend: Mitchell.

We got to know each other really well during the time we were in elementary school together. I would learn that he was in a separate classroom, just down the hall a little ways closer to the library on the second floor. Lucky him, he got to go to the second floor first! He would show me all the different toys he would bring to school, usually Lego and action figures. He and the other adults told me later on that I could participate in the Green Bean club with them, which was my school's fancy name for the recycling club. After I participated in homeroom with the rest of my classmates, I would walk down the hallway to the separate classroom. We would all then grab the outside recycling bin, walk around the building collecting the small blue bins, and take our time dumping them into the recycling dumpster. I loved that I could push the wheeled bin around the school as fast as I could, and the fact that I was also allowed to use the elevator with the secret keypad code. It was my classmate's favorite activity too, so I really had to make sure to share that giant bin.

The longer I played with Mitchell, the more confident I became to play with the other kids in the grassy area. There was a boy, much taller than Mitchell, who spoke very rarely, just like my sister when she was younger. He liked to make sounds to himself quite often, which I thought was quite beautiful. He effortlessly created a beat with all the sounds he would produce, making it easy to dance along with him under the shaded trees. There was another girl around his age who would sometimes come over to the grassy area, but she preferred to stay with the one adult I assumed she would come outside with.

The longer I played with Mitchell, the more frequently I noticed he appeared in my classes, just not like my other classmates. It almost seemed like he was part of the crowd, but very distantly. I began noticing him sitting with the same adult in specials, like music class, and especially lunch. He, along with the other students that I would see playing in the grassy patch, would sit at a table together, lumped into one section of the long, white, foldable lunch benches. Instead of being seated closer to the entrance, like in other classrooms that I would see him in, his classmates would sit close to the exit of the lunch line.

I really enjoyed spending my time with Mitchell, taking any opportunity I could to spend time with him. After one of my classmates made fun of me for always having what the school provided, and not a home-packed meal, I decided it was time to sit somewhere else. There was plenty of open room at the table with Mitchell when I asked to sit beside him. Everyone collectively scooted over in their seats so that they now took the space of two lunch benches. From that point on, I felt more comfortable sitting with the new friends I had made. I got to know the other kids quite well and even started to understand my new friends' speech. I learned that the nonverbal friends at my table communicated a lot with touch and eye gaze. If there was something that one of the two nonverbal friends wanted, they would lightly touch your shoulder and hold your hand as they guided you to something they needed or wanted to do. Some of the adults who worked with them would become frustrated when they wouldn't speak the same way I did with others, but I knew exactly what they were saying just by listening.

I would sit with Mitchell and his other friends for the rest of that year. But one day there was an incident that led to unanticipated outcomes for us. It started as any other day, with Mitchell and I sitting next to each other enjoying our lunch. At some point,

124   Love is Praxis

I don't remember exactly, Mitchell must have accidentally hurt me. It was something so trivial that my brain didn't feel the need to etch it into my memory. I yelped out, expressing that he had hurt me. He quickly came over to apologize, saying he was sorry before asking if he could give me a hug. Now, Mitchell was more than welcome to give me a hug since it was a one-and-done incident.

But this was not the case for the paraprofessional who was working with him. She quickly came over to where Mitchell and I were sitting, since she was standing somewhere else talking to the other paraprofessionals. She walked over and immediately struck him, getting too close to his face to growl at him that he had hurt me. I was stunned, not able to move for a moment as Mitchell kept attempting to hug me and apologize. The paraprofessional grabbed him, ripping him out of the lunch table. She continued to try and silence him, repeating over and over that he had hurt me. His face became splotchy with tears as he pulled from the paraprofessional's tight grasp, crying and reaching his arms out to me as I began to cry too. I continued to try and speak directly to Mitchell to calm him down, saying that I was okay and it was just an accident, while the paraprofessional continued to grab him roughly. The scene had become so theatrical at this point that the other paraprofessionals rushed over to him and practically dragged him out of the lunchroom, all while his pained cries echoed in my head, time slowing.

I never got over what I had seen that day. Every so often, the scene repeats in my head of him reaching out, screaming how he was so sorry. I felt so powerless against those adults in the room, but they were clearly hurting him. Watching that woman smack him was the most uncalled-for action I had ever witnessed, even to this day.

Right at that lunch table, as the room started to gain its noise again, I vowed that I would grow up to be that paraprofessional's boss, just to get her fired. I couldn't, wouldn't even, live knowing that someone who was supposed to be helping individuals was only causing them irreparable harm. If my teacher had done the same thing, she would have been booted out the front door. But for some reason, it was different. She continued to work with him, always aggressively handling him if he had emotions bigger than himself. He never meant any harm; he just didn't know at such a young age just how much force was too much. But even in third grade, I felt I had the responsibility to make sure that other kids didn't get treated so heinously from that point forward.

Just as it cruelly does, life continued on. Later on in my third-grade year, I began to notice that my teacher had a lot of puzzle pieces around her room. One day when we were making lanterns out of old coffee tins, she began talking about how her son has autism. That was why she was making us poke out a puzzle piece for the light to shine through our creations. We all worked carefully, making sure every detail was perfect, the shape we were creating struck me to be familiar—I remembered seeing it before.

As previously mentioned, I was nosey and loved to eavesdrop. But this also included snooping around things I wasn't supposed to. That's how I learned Santa wasn't real. But one time, when I was snooping in my mom's bedside drawer, I saw two stickers with Emma's name on them. They were those large stickers you got in the late 2000s after you visited the doctor, but hers were adorned with small animals and puzzle pieces, referencing how Emma was special. It was in that classroom that I finally made the connection that Emma truly **was** different, but she was similar to people I was already surrounded by. She wasn't different because of some horrible illness, but because she thought of things differently.

I was so intrigued by the fact that I had found someone with something similar to my sister, that I went to my teacher's desk and spilled out to her that my sister, too, had autism. My teacher expressed her amazement, eventually starting a conversation with me about my own experiences with autism. She filled in the dots for me about why Mitchell was in a separate classroom, why he wasn't in our class, but also how he was technically still a part of our grade.

As I left my third-grade homeroom, I informed my teacher that she was very likely to have my sister in class in two years. And just as I had predicted, Emma would have my third-grade teacher as her homeroom teacher as well. But their interactions didn't go the way I had anticipated. The teacher didn't treat her the same way she treated me when I was in her class. She seemed to speak slower, with a higher voice, stooping lower to the ground to address Emma. I'm pretty sure Emma was just as confused as to why this teacher was treating her so differently from her peers. I had never told her of the time I confided in that teacher about the similar diagnosis between my sister and her son.

Emma would continue to learn and grow, just like I did. She went to the same classrooms as me, had the same teachers, and worked right alongside her classmates. The only time she had to be separated from her classmates was when she began visiting the speech therapist at school. She, just like many typical third graders, had difficulty with the |r| sound. One of her goals before leaving speech therapy at the end of the year was to be able to tell my family a pirate joke.

School continued really smoothly for Emma, never showing any signs to others that she had a disability. Whenever I would tell people that my sister has autism, they immediately begin to change their tone, even to this day. They start asking questions about her as if she is suffering every single day. Then once they met her, they looked at me and quite puzzledly asked why I would lie about my sister having such a disability.

Emma and I would continue to move from grade to grade, eventually leading to another point in time where I would be at a different school from my sister. I started junior high with the rest of my classmates, including Mitchell. Being in junior high meant that we had more independence than ever before. We could walk to school, be in charge of our schedules, and would need to wake up even earlier for class! Before junior high started, my family had moved just a couple blocks away from our school district, making the walk to junior high a short ten-minute trek through alleyways. Mitchell and I had gotten to know each other so well over this time that we even started to hang out at his house. It was only a few blocks away from my house and a block away from the school. Much of my summer was spent with his family, playing outside on the trampoline or sitting in the sunroom that was converted into Mitchell's game room.

Against my best wishes, I began to learn that my home situation wasn't the norm. Dads weren't supposed to break things. Dads weren't supposed to hurt you. Dads weren't supposed to scare you. But that's what my birth father did. Learning that my life was different from others made me embarrassed. I stayed away as much as possible to avoid conflict inside my home. With Mitchell's house being so close, it became a safe haven for me to escape the unspeakable acts at home. It was almost like having two families.

A strong trust began to form between Mitchell's mom and I, to the degree that she entrusted me to walk the block back home from school with Mitchell to his house. I was to help him make a snack, take the dogs outside, wipe their paws off before letting them in, and most importantly, hang out with Mitchell. We would play Lego video games, eat pizza, watch whatever was on TV, or simply just enjoy each other's company. There was so much to do all the time, and we were just happy to spend time together.

When his mom would come home, she would greet us both the same. I would be invited to go out to dinner with them, run errands, and just participate in their lives as if I were one of their own. Their family wasn't aware for a long time why I was there so often. Their home felt safe, like I could be myself without the fear of being hurt. Mitchell's mom always remarked about how I could wolf down a plate so quickly when we were out at restaurants. She wasn't aware that the meals I shared with their family were usually the only full meals I ate in a day. I never had to worry about eating too much or being made fun of for being so skinny. I was always allowed to come over or enjoy a meal inside their home or at a restaurant. For once, in a very long time, I felt like someone important.

If there was a football game Mitchell and I were going to attend, we would also go to the afterburners together. We would dance with the other kids, listening to the DJ in a dark, dingy church run by older church members as we ate and drank the free snacks. I would become so close to their family that I was even invited to come along with them to Maryland for summer vacation. I had never gone on summer vacation at this point, especially to the beach. I was able to experience the beach for the first time with the same people who gifted me so much already. There is no physical way I will ever be able to thank that family enough for the privileges they have given me.

Most days, I would come over after school, eat a snack with Mitchell, play video games, eat dinner with his family, and then his mother would drive me back home right in time for bed. So often Mitchell's mother would cry to me, telling me how much I meant to their family, but I don't think I ever got to say it back. For all the time I refused to take payment for just sitting around the house with Mitchell, I never really got to say **thank you**. So to Brenda, thank you for creating such a safe place for me and always ensuring that I had food in my belly and was surrounded by people who loved me unconditionally. You and your family are one of the biggest reasons why I kept going when I didn't feel like I was worthy of space. You and your family are the reason I kept fighting when the future looked so dark. Because of your love, I continue to battle whatever life throws at me, knowing

130   Love is Praxis

that, just over a couple of towns, there's a group of people who care for me more than words could ever say.

The day that would forever change the course of my life happened in tenth grade during orchestra class. My mother called me, informing me that we would no longer need to live with our birth father in fear. Since he was removed from the home, we were given a second chance to discover ourselves without restriction. Specifically for Emma, it meant that she was finally able to express herself in a way that was comfortable for her. She was no longer a quiet, secretive young girl who would also be seen hiding from the rest of people. She began to talk to others openly about her beliefs, started voicing her opinions even if she thought someone wouldn't agree, and didn't keep so many secrets anymore. I was always interested in her artistic abilities, but she would never show me what was in her sketchbooks. Now, if I noticed her sketching off by herself, she would gladly show me what she was working on. She didn't need to feel ashamed anymore about developing a skill or having an interest in art.

Emma overall became a much louder person, not being afraid to take up space. Before, she would strategically go up and down our creaky wooden steps with not even a peep. Suddenly, you could always tell she was on the steps because you would hear her thunderous footsteps! She also wasn't afraid to stim in front of family, which was something I had never witnessed from her before. She had developed a sort of shiver, moving across her whole body as she would make a small wince. My mother and I learned that this was something that helped her to regulate, so we mostly ignored it. But if we did begin to tease, saying something like "Jeez! You scared me!", she didn't go back into her shell: she would laugh along with us and continue on with her day as normal.

It was quite a beautiful thing to see. I knew her so well, but it was almost like I was meeting a new person for the first time. Even now, she is extremely sociable with others and is no longer afraid to share her interests. She proudly introduces herself and informs others of her disability. She is not ashamed of her difference, but rather proud that she can be a part of such a large community that supports each other so fiercely.

Our home life affected us negatively in many ways, but it also helped us gain a better appreciation for our differences. Emma would officially be diagnosed with autism through an Autism Diagnostic Observation Schedule[16] (ADOS) at the age of 17 while I would be officially diagnosed with cPTSD, or childhood post-traumatic stress disorder. An anecdote shared by the tester performing the ADOS particularly struck me. My mother had asked him if there were any indications that my sister was affected by trauma similarly to myself. He had shared that this question was something much more difficult to answer since most autistic individuals faced daily trauma just from the efforts of masking. Because of that, identifying trauma from outside sources can be extremely difficult since the autistic brain already needs to accommodate for daily traumatic experiences.

The following year, my mother would start dating a man who is now my father. We all formed a tight familial bond from his unwavering acceptance and love that, even currently, we are eager to start the adult adoption process. The fact that he was a Registered Behavior Technician at a school for autistic individuals

132   Love is Praxis

made me respect him even more, since I could see myself right in his shoes. I am proud to be someone so affected by disability.

Since my lunch periods conflicted with Mitchell's in high school, Emma was the one who started to sit with him. They had become very close, just like Mitchell and I had. When they decided to go to prom together, I was very proud to see two of my favorite people enjoying each other's company. They would color coordinate their outfits, just like every other prom date on the floor. This would be Mitchell's senior prom, along with mine, while it was Emma's sophomore year. I also ended up going with a handful of friends and having a really memorable time. Emma had informed us that most people in her grade were going with their significant others. She didn't relate to her peers in this way, only wanting to enjoy herself with some friends instead.

Emma would later tell me that it was really important to her that she went with Mitchell because she didn't want him to be manipulated by people who truly weren't his friends. It was quite upsetting to know how many people would go around school saying they were best friends with Mitchell, but they couldn't even tell you the first thing about him. To others, he was merely a token to make them look like a considerate person. To my sister and I, he was one of the most energetic, kindest, and most interesting people to hold a conversation with. From the pictures I would see afterward, the two of them had a fantastic time together, and I'm really glad they were able to have such a memorable event together.

At the time of writing, I am in the final year of my bachelor's course in special education at Penn State University, hoping to eventually earn my master's degree and complete studies on how autism is identified for women and girls. Every day, I am motivated to keep striving hard for the individuals I have worked with during this program, the people I have learned from, and the people I have been learning with. I am forever grateful for the opportunities that have been given to me during this time, all because I found my path working in the disability community.

As I reflect on my life experiences in the community, I recognize certain signs in me that made me consider the fact that I may also be an individual with neurodivergence. During times when I am skeptical of an ADHD diagnosis, my sister would comment that, more and more, people with ADHD and autism are seen as getting along well. Neurodivergence simply just finds neurodivergence, in a way that people follow the path of discovering their own people.

One of the things I find most interesting while working alongside people in the disability community is the discussion of labels: are they needed and are they necessary? Particularly for my sister, her suspected label of autism assisted her with early intervention services. For Mitchell, his life was set on a path of Individualized Education Plans (IEPs) and separate classrooms because of the so-called severity of his diagnosis. My belief is that the labeling process can only do as much for you depending on your needs. I think it is extremely important to not only address possible developmental delays but also give young children open access to educational resources as soon as possible. Children show the most success when they are exposed to academics as early as three years of age. Most commonly, a label can provide a family with reassurance, services, and support. But if these factors are not desired by the family unit, a label can just be used to further isolate an individual from their peers. As much as I would like the world to focus on how differences are simply that, our society has developed a system that differences must be addressed.

But the change starts at the first level. Ensure that the people around you are treated with the same respect, kindness, and grace, no matter their individual markers. We are all discovering this life for the first time. It should not take the explicit conversation of someone saying they have a disability to earn respect; respect should be the first gift you give to someone.

Reflective questions

1. How does the author describe their own views of difference? How does this compare with views of difference among other people they have encountered?

2. Even though Emma and Mitchell have the same diagnosis of autism, what do their experiences tell you about disability "profiles"?

3. What does the author mean regarding Emma no longer having to mask at home? What function do you think masking served in their home environment?

4. What are your thoughts about the reasons why Emma decided to go to the prom with Mitchell? What are some efforts your school takes to promote authentic relationships for students with disabilities?

5. According to the author, what may be a reason why a person seeks out a disability label? How does this conflict or conform to your position on labels?

10
School as a Site of Resistance: Becoming an Advocate

Azaria Cunningham

> School is a site of pain
> The flames of advocacy exist
> But for who, when, and at what risk?
> What can school districts and teachers do?
> What can teacher preparation programs and
> teacher educators do?
> What can you do?
> School is a site of resistance

Reflecting back as a Black woman pre-service teacher at a predominately white institution (PWI), I felt like I had to grin and bear it. There were instances across programs (science courses and education courses) when I was "the only one". I felt like I had to make myself small because I had a hypervisible presence. It is similar to when you are taking a state exam in an incredibly silent lecture hall and you drop your pen. The sound travels through

136   Love is Praxis

the room like a falling body, and everyone turns to stare at you. I experienced a sense of scrutiny every time I entered a classroom. I surmised that the hypervisibility came about due to my racial and gender identity. Often, I remember these moments and wonder about my voice, stance, and positionality. In truth, it was nonexistent. As a prospective teacher, my primary concerns revolved around effectively instructing students, mitigating potential conflicts with parents, and successfully passing the Praxis exam[17].

My advocacy journey began as a teacher, but I wish it had started as an undergraduate student. Upon reflection, I wish that my professors in my teacher preparation program (TPP) modeled or planted the seed of advocacy within me. However, the advocacy ignited when I had to be a fence between the administration at my place of employment, Shark Middle School (SMS; pseudonym), and my students. I hope that by sharing my story, I can dispel any notion that having emergent bilingual students and students with disabilities is inherently problematic. Rather, I aim to highlight how white supremacy patriarchy manifests within the system and among those in power.

I taught science at SMS for five years for grades six through eight. I remember vividly receiving all the classes with students with disabilities and emergent bilinguals (García *et al.*, 2008). Initially, when the school administration handed me the roster during the staff meeting at the beginning of the year, I thought nothing of it. That was until my white teaching counterpart, Stacy, showed me her schedule for all general science classes—something snapped and rose up inside of me. I had questions and felt angry due to the clearly biased scheduling. At that moment,

I confronted my principal about the schedules and asked why I had all the classes of students receiving either special education or English language support. My principal looked me dead in the eye and replied, "Because you can handle it." I silently pondered, so Stacy couldn't handle it—why was this constantly my narrative? Is it because I am **Black**?

Then, I mustered the strength to respond.

"How is this schedule fair to me or the students?"

The principal replied, "Well, you know you handle students' behavior really well, and Stacy can't."

Again, silently, I pondered, *is it my problem that she cannot strategize how to manage her classroom or constantly send students to my class*? *As an administrator, shouldn't you provide opportunities for staff to develop their pedagogy to be inclusive of all student needs*? I take a deep breath and say, "I understand that, but will I be given the support (e.g. bilingual teacher support or in-class support paraprofessional) to meet my students' needs?" My principal quickly replied, "Of course." Later, I found out it was a lie; however, at that moment, I felt like I accomplished something and, for once, heard. But in reality, the principal's agreement was to appease me for that one instance and get me out of his office.

The reality was that the school district did not provide adequate special education services or support for English language learners. The district mainly offered special education services for students in English Language Arts and Mathematics, which were state-tested subject areas. Student Individualized Educational

Plans (IEPs) are tailored to these specific subjects. As a result, students were not serviced in Science, Social Studies, and other electives, even though in some IEPs, students had accommodations listed. The school district blamed the discrepancy for not receiving services, primarily due to insufficient funds or staff shortages. Parents who knew their children's IEP rights brought cases against the school district while others struggled silently. I remember feeling like my students' parents' voices held more weight than mine and that we should partner against the district.

Beyond this situation, I had a few painful memories of my students feeling ostracized by the general education teachers and students. My students would tell me how they felt treated differently during recess and lunch periods, where adults spoke down to them or yelled at them. When my students reacted due to this mistreatment, they were further punished for not "respecting" adults. Studies have reported how students with disabilities and emergent bilinguals have been subjected to disproportionate punishment and discipline in schools (Bal *et al.*, 2019; Boyce, 2020). The label for students with disabilities and emergent bilinguals was a label that not only followed my students in the classroom but also during lunch. My students were homogeneously grouped and placed into their classes based on test scoring and identification (e.g. emergent bilingual). In the cafeteria, my students were all seated in the same area at the back, nearest to the wall. Students were segregated based on their classes and could not move around freely, which became a stigma for them and a source of mistreatment. Tatum's (1997) *Why Are All the Black Kids Sitting Together in the Cafeteria?* talks about students self-segregating due to racial and ethnic identities. The seating segregation patterns at Shark Middle School were similar, with the only distinction being that my students were forced to sit according to the school's categorization.

When my students relayed their experiences, I confronted the adults in the cafeteria. I challenged the seating arrangement by physically sitting with my students and allowing them to sit with their friends in general education classes. Becoming a teacher advocate means being a fence, meaning you are the only line of defense and voice between the system and the student. Reflecting on these experiences, I want to consider ways school districts and teachers can create inclusive, safe spaces for students. In addition, I want to explore how TPP can introduce possibilities for empowering future teachers to develop their advocacy stances.

What can school districts and teachers do?

Over the years, I realized that the experiences I mentioned are not isolated instances that occur against students with disabilities and emergent bilingual students. As a result, I believe considerations should be made such as training for staff (e.g. paraprofessionals, lunch monitors, teachers, etc.) working in the school setting to be inclusive and anti-deficit. The lack of understanding and support for students' needs, coupled with their own racist, linguistic, and disability biases, results in punishments that are often committed by school staff who are in direct contact with students. The district and building administration must build relationships (e.g. team building) among all teachers. There is a stigma that not only resides in the student's experience but also within the teacher's sphere. The special and general education teachers have trouble understanding their roles within the classroom and the possibilities for collaboration. School districts and building administrations can not only expect this but must also intentionally create opportunities for co-planning time between general and special education teachers.

Going beyond just theoretical ideas and discussions, which occur only at the surface level, there needs to be a show of commitment and a stake in the progress of students with disabilities. Developing collaborative learning communities provides support not only to the needs of the student but also to the needs of the staff members. Providing professional development on co-teaching models can lead to a collaborative culture where all learners have the opportunity to have an equitable learning and schooling experience. In addition, administrators should consider how biased scheduling affects teachers as well as the students they service. Yes, we can handle it, but at the same time, at what cost? The strong Black woman trope is exhaustive and dehumanizing in the schooling environment.

What can TPPs and teacher educators do?

TPPs should ensure that they indoctrinate teacher educators and future teachers about asset-based approaches and the rights of learners. For many, schools can be a site of violence rather than a space for learning. As TPPs and teacher educators responsible for preparing future teachers, it is imperative that the curriculum exposes future teachers to the realities of the classroom while developing their advocacy stance—an advocacy stance for themselves as future educators as well as how to advocate for their prospective students. To help facilitate these conversations, teacher educators can introduce case studies, for example, books such as *Case Studies on Diversity and Social Justice Education* (Gorski and Pothini, 2013). Gorski and Pothini's book provides racist, sexist, and ableist real-world scenarios on issues of social justice and educational equity that both pre-service and in-service teachers can examine and reflect upon.

Schools as a site for resistance

> To educate as the practice of freedom is a way of teaching that anyone can learn. That learning process comes easiest to those of us who teach who also believe that there is an aspect of our vocation that is sacred; who believe that our work is not merely to share information but to share in the intellectual and spiritual growth of our students. To teach in a manner that respects and cares for the souls of our students is essential if we are to provide the necessary conditions where learning can most deeply and intimately begin. (hooks, 1994, p. 13)

In my reflection on bell hooks' seminal work *Teaching to Transgress*, I find a resonance between her work and my own experiential insights as an educator. Central to hooks' pedagogical philosophy is the notion of education as a practice of freedom, wherein cultivating liberatory learning environments is contingent upon recognizing and prioritizing students' well-being. This resonates profoundly with my endeavors to foster a pedagogical space characterized by respect, care, and empowerment. hooks

142   Love is Praxis

advocates an educational praxis that goes beyond simply transmitting information and, instead, emphasizes a pedagogical approach that is highly attuned to the intellectual and spiritual development of students.

My decision to engage and take a stance with students beyond the confines of the traditional classroom, symbolized by the act of sitting with them in the cafeteria, epitomizes a commitment to nurturing meaningful connections and fostering trust. By affording students the autonomy to move freely within the cafeteria space, I sought to dismantle oppressive structures that often permeate educational settings, echoing hooks' criticism of institutionalized education. In addition, hooks' examination of power dynamics in educational systems strongly aligns with my recognition of the failures perpetuated by the administration, colleagues, and the system. Through my recognition of these systemic barriers and my proactive efforts to challenge them, I strived to create an educational environment where all students could feel liberated, which should be everyone's goal. This aligns with hooks' call to disrupt hegemonic paradigms and cultivate critical inquiry and transformative learning spaces.

In conclusion, my experiences as an educator reflect a convergence with bell hooks' pedagogical philosophy, particularly her advocacy for education as a site of liberation and empowerment. Through embodying the values of freedom, respect, and care espoused by hooks, I aim to contribute to the creation of educational spaces that honor the dignity, humanity, and agency of all learners. My experiences shared as an educator are not a monolith. Issues within the special education and emergent bilingual experiences will persist until all parties involved in student learning—including families, administrators, teacher educators, teachers, and programs that prepare teachers—take a stand for educational equity.

What can you do? With the aim of disrupting how we perpetuate a system of marginalization, I've created a few questions for you to reflect on.

Reflective questions

1. What does advocacy look like for you in the past, present, and future?
2. What are some ways that you can think of to advocate for your student's needs?
3. How can you plant the seed of advocacy within your students, parents, and community?
4. As a teacher, how do you ensure the rights of the learner?
5. As a teacher, how do you collaborate with your administration and school system to create actionable steps that adhere to student IEPs?
6. As a teacher educator, how do you teach your pre-service teachers to collaborate with their future administration and school system to create actionable steps that adhere to student IEPs?

11

Empowering Exceptionality: A Mother's Call for Collaborative Understanding in Education

Ruby Humphris

My journey to motherhood began in a rather typical way. I had some physical signs that pointed to a potential pregnancy, some food and smell aversions, and of course my missing menstrual cycle for the month of October 2022. I ran to the store to buy a home pregnancy test to confirm my suspicions. In the fall of 2002, it is odd to say but, "Googling" symptoms was not as ubiquitous as they are now. Instead, I called my best friend on a landline telephone and shared with her that the only food that sounded palatable to me over the past two weeks had been bananas and a Burger King Original Chicken Sandwich. I counted five whole minutes in my head, one, one thousand, two, two thousand, and so on. I can remember distinctly how I felt looking at those two pink lines staring back at me. My heart quickened. ***Was I ready to be a mom? Would I know how to feed a baby and change their diaper? Maybe the test was a false positive? Would my baby have my eyes and their father's laugh?*** What I did not consider was whether my child would be neurotypical or not. Would my child be medically complex, or would I have to dive headfirst into an advocacy role that my 20 years of life thus far had not prepared me for. I stared in wonderment at impossibly small socks and onesies and envisioned my child's "typical life".

No rest for the weary

The truth is I was not prepared to navigate a life with my son Jimi that included a list of diagnoses that were both cognitive and medical. My schema this far included an understanding of child development that was more normative. Jimi arrived rather quietly four months before his expected day of delivery via induction of labor because of my severe preeclampsia, later eclampsia, and placenta previa. He and I had both become rather unwell during that final month of pregnancy. The maternal fetal medicine team of doctors proclaimed that on that very day in June at that very hour I would be sent to labor and delivery to be induced. After a very difficult labor, where Jimi and I fought for our lives and needed to be resuscitated several times each, Jimi endured a birth injury and head/brain trauma that later resulted in some neurodivergence, cognitive differences, and medical complexities that meant that his physical, mental, and emotional development would not follow the trajectory that "most" children follow.

My son Jimi did not reach the milestones that were listed on the monthly questionnaire that the pediatrician's office thrust into our hands as parents at every monthly well-child visit. He did not roll over "on time"; he didn't sit up unassisted "on time"; he didn't walk, "on time". Jimi did not sleep well. In fact, nighttime was the most challenging time of the day. He had severely disturbed sleep, which included acute central sleep apnea, and I paced the living room floor for miles and miles each night in a vain attempt to get Jimi to rest since I knew his brain development depended on that rest. I remember feeling defeated as a mother. There was a list a mile long that spoke to all the things he was not doing, but nothing that spoke to what he could do, what he liked, or who he was. I remember feeling much of the language used to describe my son and his abilities was subtractive. It was most certainly not person first language. When people use language that puts the person before their diagnosis, they are using person first language by describing that a person has a condition as opposed to being a condition. For example, when individuals say a student "is" ADHD to relay a diagnosis, they are consciously or subconsciously marginalizing and dehumanizing that student by failing to mentally separate the person from the diagnosis, which reinforces a notion that the person and their diagnosis are inherently bad or inferior. This leads to further stigma and discrimination, while also implicitly perpetuating this notion of inferiority. When person first language is used, we avoid essentializing the condition as the primary identity of the individual.

Jimi's communication: a mother's understanding

By the time Jimi was two years old I felt like a failure as a mother. People would mutter and stare at him when he had a tantrum or if he gazed into the distance while having a seizure. He did not offer the usual babble that most infants do. He did not utter "mama" or "dada" as a six-month-old, and at two years of age, he gave very little, if any, eye contact and did not verbalize words. He did however communicate. He used gestures, he used utterances, and he smiled. I do not recall anyone asking me about his other modes of communication; I just remember people asking me if I was worried that he didn't speak yet. Worried was not the correct word; I just wanted to make sure he could communicate his needs and wants with all the people in his life. We did not know in the first year of his life what the long-term implications of his birth injury might entail. As Jimi's disabilities were a result of his birth injury, all the medical community could do was offer their best guess. He may be "wheelchair bound", or he may "have the mental age of an eight-year-old". You see, even 21 years ago the language was still very deficit-based (Connor and Ferri, 2005). I felt providers were not seeing the whole child. Words do carry an immense amount of weight. I was happy that, at the age of two, he handed me his sippy cup when he wanted some water, and that, the week before this, I had successfully managed to brush his hair without tears. For me, these were huge successes.

Jimi was diagnosed as having an intellectual disability (IDD), cerebral palsy (CP), and autism spectrum disorder (ASD), all within his second and third years of life. He was involved in feeding, occupational, physical, and vision therapies. I felt we spent more hours in the day at the doctor's and therapists' offices than at home. My son Max was born 12 months after Jimi's birthday, and I must say that when Max was surpassing Jimi in every milestone, my concern for Jimi's communication began to escalate. I pushed the pediatrician for a referral for an evaluation with the speech and language therapist. We were on the waiting list for just shy of six months.

Jimi qualified for services as I had assumed he would due to having no verbal speech by the time he was two years and ten months old. I was not aware that some children never acquire spoken words. I was not an expert; I just knew the other children in the mommy and me classes we attended were developing vocabulary. No one was trying to communicate with him through sign or augmentative and alternative communication (AAC), and to be honest, it felt like a hidden menu I was not privy to. I did not know what AAC was; I did not know what to ask for or how to help my child communicate. I was hopeful that the speech and language pathologist (SLP) would help us, that she would crack the code, that the voice inside my son would finally be heard. Unfortunately, after just two sessions with her, she called us into the office to discharge Jimi from services because he would not make eye contact with her and would not engage or speak with her; hence, there was nothing more she could do for us. I walked out of the office shocked and bewildered. I had tears in my eyes. I did not know what I would need to do, but I knew I would walk to the ends of the earth for my child. This very moment was a defining one for me not only as a mother but also as an advocate

Professional gaze: failed understandings

I wish at this point in our story I could say that this was the only roadblock or challenge Jimi experienced. The truth is that this experience was the first of many that followed in his 21 years of life thus far. I have lost count of the number of times that members of the medical and school communities painted me as an unreasonable and loud mother. My driving force was to obtain equitable participation for my child in all areas of life and within his community. I realized that it was easier to stay quiet and accept what we were told and directed. However, surrender and acceptance were not what was best for my child. I knew he needed interventions that were culturally and socially meaningful to him. I knew that what I requested was not unreasonable. I armed myself with data and became a part of a rich community of individuals with varied disabilities and their families.

It appeared that this experience was not unique. Time and time again, mothers and fathers shared their experiences with me regarding how they felt unheard, unseen, and as though their opinion was not asked, and it did not matter. Some families felt that they were not being communicated with effectively; the only point of contact they had in their childrens' schools didn't speak their primary language and getting an interpreter was nearly impossible. Some parents had disabilities themselves and their preferred means of communication was not facilitated by their childrens' schools or medical providers. We as parents know our children best. We are their first teachers; we are their safe place. We know their strengths and where they need the most support.

This is not to say that as parents we don't acknowledge professional expertise. We certainly appreciate that doctors, therapists, and educators have spent countless hours and years in their courses of study and have developed a level of general expertise in their fields. However, in my own professional and personal experience, I have learned that the best outcomes for children come from truly collaborative teams that include parental input. I can share that when I have worked with families in a professional context what resonates is my shared lived experiences as a parent with a child with a disability as well as welcoming their input and trying to facilitate and incorporate their vision and requests for support for their children, instead of creating an atmosphere where they feel they are being unreasonable. Even the most seemingly unreasonable parental requests come from a place of support and concern for the well-being of their child (Zeitlin and Curcic, 2014).

Reframing it: beyond a disability label

If I could share a message with special educators as a mother of a child who has more comprehensive support needs and more complex medical needs, it would be to recognize my child is more than the data, more than his diagnosis. We have different concerns for our children at different ages and stages. Remember to work with us, and not **against** us. Know that we are aware of all the factors affecting each of our student's performance in your classroom. Let us work with you. I may be loud because I am frustrated that I have not been heard. I may seem unreasonable because I emailed you five times about the same concern, but it is because my child is important to me. Yes, parents need to meter their expectations, and teachers must create boundaries for their classroom and familial engagement that allow for an equitable work-life balance for them. But if you speak to us as a collaborator, as part of the IEP team, we are willing to listen.

Watch what words you use when speaking about our children. Do not just tell us all they are doing "wrong" or what they cannot yet do. Framing our children's abilities from a strengths-based perspective is so helpful. Try not to use statements such as "he is ADHD", "he is autistic, it's ok, he doesn't understand", or "he is wheelchair bound". All these statements are subtractive, and they elicit a feeling that as educators you only see the deficits first. My child is so much more than his exceptionality. When you hear other members of the faculty use similar language, please correct them—these changes need to happen from the ground up. If you hear it, reframe it. Remember we all have the same goal; we are all putting so much effort into the cultivation of those children that comprise your classroom. Let's build truly holistic collaborative spaces that are inclusive and representative of a diverse classroom community.

Thank you for choosing to educate my child. I can count on one hand the number of educators who truly made a difference in my son's life. Jimi recently graduated from high school with a diploma and spends his weekdays in a community work program facilitated by work coaches who were once educators themselves. I will forever be grateful to the educators who chose to see and educate the whole student.

Reflective questions

1. How will you communicate to parents that their input is valuable and will be used to create measurable goals for their students?

2. What can you do to create culturally relevant and meaningful differentiated instruction for your students that invites them to use all methods of communication available to them?

3. Have you examined your own implicit biases and how they may affect the way you engage with your students and their families?

4. How will you show your students that they are safe and loved in your classroom—a space that they will spend the majority of their day in?

12
Kerri's Way: Family, Lessons, and Memoir

Courtney Kehoe

Ever since I was two years old, I have been surrounded by varying means of accessing the world. Although it was complex to me at the time, and still is today, I thought everyone's grandpop knew seizure protocol, played in sensory bins, and clung by the side of their older sister. I ate with a fork and knife, and she ate with a feeding tube. I trotted around, while she used a wheelchair. Within the realms of my family and my home, this was just the way it was, and I thought nothing of it. I loved my life this way, and this was just another day. In my eyes, every family had an experience like this.

My older sister, Kerri, is a very sassy and pleasant girl. She is quick to roll her eyes at someone she does not want to see, but she smiles through medical hardships. She loves to laugh, spend time with her sisters, and watch her cousins get in trouble. Her presence lights up every room.

Kerri has a diagnosis of an intellectual disability (ID). She was diagnosed with microcephaly, epilepsy, a cortical visual impairment, and a diaphragmatic hernia at only six weeks old. She received surgery upon this diagnosis to alleviate some of the medical stress exerted on her body. Her symptoms manifest through low muscle tone, difficulties in fine motor skills, difficulty eating and swallowing, difficulties producing vocalizations, and frequent, severe seizures. She receives outpatient physical therapy, occupational therapy, speech therapy, vision therapy, at-home teaching, and at-home nursing services. My family, overwhelmed by having to care for an infant, toddler, and child with complex needs, sought help and coordinated care through an external organization in Philadelphia.

Kerri: a family and individual disability experience

Intellectual disability has been a reality for me, Kerri, and my family since Kerri was an infant. Kerri's diagnosis, microcephaly, is defined as abnormally small head size in relation to one's age. This ultimately manifests as intellectual disability, inherently causing a developmental delay that affects several areas causing problems with fine and gross motor skills, feeding and swallowing, vision, speech, and many more. These persisted throughout her childhood. Kerri uses a wheelchair for mobility and received services to assist with other affected areas of development.

The developmental milestones Kerri will reach occur at a much slower rate than those of her nondisabled or nonlabelled peers. Due to the prevalence of low muscle tone, my family and I found ourselves celebrating more basic milestones that would not be of merit to other families. Taking a step, holding a spoon, and being seizure-free for a day were reasons for lots of cheering and happiness in my house. Owing to the frequency of her seizures,

Kerri was on the ketogenic diet upon request of her neurologist at the Children's Hospital of Philadelphia (CHOP). This diet is said to alleviate the prevalence and severity of Kerri's seizures, it but was extremely unappetizing for her. I remember watching as she would cringe at the high-fat dinners and desserts she would have to eat.

Beyond the diagnosis

Kerri is extremely honest. When someone with whom she is familiar enters the room, they would know immediately how she feels about their presence just by the look on her face. If she does not want to see you, you will receive quite an attitude and some stubbornness. She is someone who knows exactly what she wants and does not want, which is impressive for such a young girl. Kerri is also very loving to her family, friends, and support systems. Her endearing smile and laugh are infectious and can light up any room. Her favorite stuffed animals are a soft brown monkey and a rainbow caterpillar that she loves to have with her during unpleasant doctor visits. Due to her compromised immune system and young age, she has not been in a school around other children yet, but her best buddies are her little sister and Pop-pop.

Our immediate family consists of Kerri, me, my little sister, Allison, and my mom and dad. When Kerri was sick, my mom worked part-time to stay home with her as much as she could and maintain a work-life balance. My father works full-time but is very involved with Kerri, playing and spending time with her whenever he gets the opportunity. My grandparents love Kerri very much, and they are deeply involved in all aspects of her life. My grandpop, who watched my siblings and me throughout the day while my parents were working, was informed of seizure protocol, and he was always unafraid to step into action when seizures arose. My grandparents also spent a significant amount of time with Kerri in the hospital and also provided respite care to Alli and me during these times.

In a world that is created to accommodate only nondisabled people, Kerri and our family face many societal barriers. Many people who do not know Kerri or her family well are likely to make assumptions about Kerri's abilities, or lack thereof, as well as question her mom's health and carefulness during her pregnancy with Kerri.

Although individuals with microcephaly share many similar manifestations to those of Kerri, not everyone who has this diagnosis experiences it the same way. Some individuals may experience only some, whereas others experience more manifestations in a more significant/comprehensive/complex manner and may need more support throughout their lifespan. For individuals with increased manifestations, professionals may set goals to optimize the life experiences of the individual while they are young, helping them to enjoy school and time with their family. This was the reality for Kerri. The goal of each day was to ensure that she went to sleep happy, as we were unsure how much time she would spend here with us.

Kerri is the reason

On a bitterly cold February day, in 2006, Kerri passed away from the flu when she was only six years old. I was three years old then.

With a weakened immune system, she could not fight the virus. From day one, she was my best friend. My being apart from her at naptime turned into being apart forever. At this point in my life, as a toddler, the concept of death was so foreign to me. I frequently asked my mom where Kerri was and when she would be coming back. To this, my mom, frozen in time to that say, would softly respond "Heaven" each time. The Christmas after her passing, when I sat on Santa's lap, I wished for him to stop there first to make sure Kerri would receive her Christmas presents.

Kerri's impact

In the field of education, after a difficult day in the classroom, it is easy to sit at your desk and ask yourself, "Why?" Within the triumphs and pitfalls educators and students face together daily, it is easy to lose sight of why we do what we do. I urge you, when this happens in practice, to remember my story, like I do so often. Kerri is my "why", the reason I am an emerging special educator. I chose to focus on her, as she was someone any teacher would have loved to have in their classroom. I look forward to establishing close-knit relationships with my students, like the relationships Kerri's support team developed with her. I hope to become someone my students feel comfortable coming to with any problems they face or victories they want to celebrate; I hope to be someone that maintains this relationship even after students leave my classroom, acting as a resource for my students and their families as much as I possibly can across the lifespan.

Questions from a pre-service educator

Because Kerri would have been preparing to transition into public school, I was curious about how the transition process into kindergarten is carried out for students exiting early intervention and who are eligible for continued academic services. I was also drawn to researching what services are available for emotionally supporting parents and families through this transition. This can be a very difficult time not only for the child but their caretakers as well. Through my research, I have learned that this process may differ from state to state. I was unable to find significant research on this specific transitional process; however, the Pennsylvania Department of Education provided substantial information regarding students in Pennsylvania who are of age to transition to kindergarten. Parents are given the opportunity to withhold entry into kindergarten to give their child an opportunity to remain in preschool for another year. According to both IDEA and Rous and Hallam's "Transitions Services for Young Children with Disabilities: Research and Future Practices", transitioning into kindergarten is not addressed in IDEA. The lack of emphasis in this area makes advocacy that much more important for special educators. Entering grade school is a monumental step for students and families, especially for students with disabilities, and the lack of support in this area is concerning for children and families in need. Their article provides areas of focus when considering transition planning, such as family visits to the child's future school, home visits from teachers before and after school entry, gradual transitioning with specific goals and objectives, and the importance of communication with parents. My family would have greatly benefitted from each of these individual activities, they were very worried about Kerri entering kindergarten within the next year.

Another question I sought to answer about ID and Kerri's specific experience with schooling is how the medical manifestations of Kerri's diagnosis will be handled in the academic setting. She is on many medications as well as a special diet to better manage her seizures, and the individuals currently equipped to handle her medical needs are her parents, grandparents, and nurses. I can imagine that this would be a concern for parents of children with specific medical needs, so I was curious about how these needs are met outside of the home or hospital. Through my research, I found that students with medical manifestations are assigned a nurse who will administer any medication or handle any medical emergency that may arise. In the article titled "Caring for a Child with a Life-Limiting Condition: The Experiences of Nurses in an Intellectual Disability Service Provider", Connor and Corcoran (2022) describe the way in which staffing shortages bring about difficulties when medical emergencies surface. However, their findings emphasized the close-knit relationship that nurses develop with the individuals for whom they care. Kerri and her family have found this to be very true in their own lives. One of her at-home nurses has become very close with Kerri's mom, and they consider each other very good friends.

In addition to transition services and nursing services outside of the home, I had a question regarding how students with ID experience school and how I as a teacher of exceptional learners can enhance the experiences of my students with this label. The sources I found provided compelling and empowering tactics to enhance my students' scholastic experiences. Uplifting students' voices in the classroom is of utmost importance to make them feel empowered and confident with academic material (Bayes et al., 2013). Students should also be given individualized, scaffolded supports in the classroom, aiding in developing a strong teacher-student relationship. These relationships have the power to alter student perspectives on school, increasing their excitement to learn and grow. The classroom is a place wherein students should feel safe and comfortable, and such relationships, as well as the classroom environment, make this possible for all students. Involving parents in the classroom dynamic and keeping them in the know about their child's successes at school help enhance the academic experience for students with ID. Further, encouraging community involvement for students is said to improve their experiences at school (Malapela and Thupayagale-Tshweneagae, 2024).

Intellectual disability is a category often centered around deficits—what individuals cannot do. The IDEA, which is the pinnacle of modern special education, describes ID as "significantly subaverage general intellectual functioning", which inherently compares individuals with ID to their nondisabled peers in a way that discounts their strengths (Sec. 300.8 (c)(6), IDEA, 2004). This is an unfair connection that may potentially evoke bias against those with ID[18] due to the prevalence of this law in our society. As a pre-service teacher preparing to support students with ID in my future classroom, the deficit-focused attitudes surrounding ID and disability are disheartening and frightening. With that said, support and advocacy are integral.

Conclusion

Kerri's way is similar to those of so many individuals and families across the globe. As I prepare to become a practicing special educator, I look forward to relishing opportunities to build relationships with my students and their families, empower identity, and remember my "why".

Reflective questions

1. Reflect on tight-knit relationships between family members. As an educator, how can you work to ensure all family and team members feel heard and valued?
2. How can you empower your students and their families to feel informed in their decision-making, without letting your personal biases infiltrate?
3. How can you help students who are not in your classroom form relationships with individuals with more complex needs?

13
The System Failed Me, but I Did Not Personally Fail

Jenna Spencer

Many people grow up with challenging events in life, and I was no different. In this country, there are systems established to protect people, but the system put in place for individuals with disabilities is outdated and filled with ableism, which made my experience in the schools incredibly difficult and, at times, very lonely. Growing up receiving special education services from the time I was six I had to encounter several ableist professionals and a system that failed me, as well as many others. The system is continuing to fail students with disabilities which is why I advocate through telling my story, using my voice, and being a guest speaker sharing some experiences.

Set up to fail

From a young age, my parents noticed I had challenges that my other siblings did not. They noticed from an early age that I was developmentally behind, especially in speech and in fine and gross motor skills. They also noticed I had some sensory challenges as well as fixations. So they decided to push for tests. From that point on I was always at the doctor's offices, getting MANY tests or receiving therapies. Every test led to another incorrect diagnosis, and still, we were not getting any closer to understanding why I was struggling. My parents expressed their concerns to multiple doctors including specialists, only to be dismissed saying I just had a learning gap because of being adopted and to just be patient. My mom just knew it was more than that. After all, a mother always knows right? My parents saw the signs and tried to get professionals to take them seriously, but the professionals continuously blamed it on circumstances and presented diagnoses that were just wrong.

Before elementary school, the signs my parents noticed were mainly speech delay and fine and gross motor challenges. The speech delay alone should have afforded me speech therapy or an early intervention evaluation at the least. Instead, my parents were dismissed by professionals, and this had consequences. I did not receive any services until elementary school. Since I did not say words until I was two years old, the question still stands 21 years later: why were my family's valid concerns dismissed? This left my parents feeling at a loss, for they knew something was going on but did not have the support to know where to turn to get help. They felt helpless, knowing that I needed extra help and support, yet nobody took them seriously. My parents were left not knowing where to turn.

At Penn State, particularly in the major of special education, we talk a lot about how the earlier such students get intervention, the better it is for them because they won't have as many significant challenges in these areas for a longer period (ECTA, 2011).

The system failed me, but I did not personally fail 167

Early intervention also provides support to the family. So why was my family treated differently? Why was my family not given the support they deserved, and why were they disregarded time after time? These professionals could have chosen to acknowledge my family's concerns and evaluate me so that I could have received the appropriate help and diagnosis sooner. Instead, we were dismissed and I was set up to fail. How is it that as a country we pride ourselves on the amazing services and support, yet if you don't have the "typical look" you are set up to fail? Does that sound like an amazing and supportive system that you want your child to grow up in?

I sure would not want my child to grow up in such a system. I want my children to grow up in a system where they are supported, valued, and set up to succeed. I have just recently reached a point in my life where I've overcome this system and defied people's expectations. Despite the sad reality of having to prove people wrong in the first place, it was extremely rewarding. I got to show them they were wrong—me, a successful student, soon-to-be author, and emerging teacher.

It comes as no surprise that growing up I was always confused and felt like an outsider. I felt like I was always **that** girl and stood out in the wrong ways. In middle school, my mental health started to decline. I was having challenges with family dynamics and became very annoyed at every little thing and was feeling embarrassed for receiving special education services. As things got worse and we were no closer to a diagnosis, my parents and doctors thought it would be helpful to receive a higher level of care. I was then admitted to a partial hospital program. Around this time, teachers and doctors started to play with the idea of me possibly having autism. Every time I heard the word **autism**, I thought I was hearing things. I could not believe they assumed that just because I played with my hair. I was tested for autism in the sixth grade. However, we did not get the results until the end of seventh grade.

A system not made for me

It wasn't until I was thirteen that I finally got the autism diagnosis. After the diagnosis, people always told my family that this was a good thing and that I qualified for many services. My family quickly learned that despite the services offered, the system was still not made for me; rather, it was actually created by and for people without disabilities. Although we do have good services for those requiring intensive support, we still live in a world where people believe having a disability is a bad thing. Until the perceptions about disability change, the system will continue to fail students. We will continue to have students with high needs receiving good support while a child in the same school will be left lost with a lack of support because of a simple number on an IQ test. I was diagnosed, told about all the "amazing" services that can be availed, thrown into an autistic support classroom, and then left to figure it out, all while struggling with mental health and the denial of the diagnosis.

After the autism diagnosis, everything changed around me, and within me. My family expected a quality education and individualized support. However, while the teachers addressed my academic challenges, it felt like none of my mental health challenges were ever brought up. Instead of supporting my mental health, I was met with countless professionals with very ableist views, who continued to tell me everything I couldn't do. As a result, my mental health and self-esteem deteriorated. Nobody ever felt the need to address my mental health after my autism diagnosis. Maybe they just thought that because I have autism I would not have that struggle because of a lack of feelings. Well, guess what? I do have feelings and empathy, so when they avoided helping me with mental health, it caused more harm than good. Studies have also proven that this is a myth and a stereotypical view of autism(Hume and Burgess, 2021). Since I was diagnosed late, I went through five years of denial and hating the word autism when people were referring to my disability. There were days when I would cringe when someone would talk about my autism, and on others, I would actually cry. In eighth grade, when I told my classmate that I had autism, all I could remember was her facial expression: her eyes widened as she stared at me in pure shock. For someone who had already absolutely hated having this label, her reaction just made it so much worse. I went from just hating the label to hating everything about myself, becoming so fixated on trying just to find ways to be "normal". I went as far as Googling medications and surgeries for autism. When I was diagnosed, I would pray for the autism to go away and hope that this was just a terrible dream.

When "help" is actually harm: take one

Throughout the education process, I had different support teams that would try to "help" me succeed. Some were good, others were bad, but the worst was definitely in high school. I imagine my team thought they were helping me, but it did more harm than good. When you get told everything you can't do at least twice a year, those words consume your entire world as well as your self-worth. I felt like I had no control or say in my educational decisions, or how these professionals viewed me. This devastated me because their opinion held so much value to me. To hear that they did not believe in me broke me. I just wanted to be seen as me, Jenna, for once, with no labels or expectations.

Not only was there harm from the school personnel, but from the day I got the diagnosis, my own peers started to treat me differently. As seen through my classmates' reactions, I was suddenly known only for my diagnosis and not for who I was as a person. Only a few months after receiving my diagnosis, when I was still trying to accept it, I was cyberbullied. This lasted for months, as the bullies attacked the very part of me that I was most insecure about. They decided to make fun of how I spoke, called me "stupid", and guessed what disability I had. It started with them just laughing at how I looked or talked. Later they would share pictures with each other and say things like "Who are these people?", and someone would reply with "Probably her autistic support group?" For someone who already had a lot of shame and embarrassment regarding my disability, you can imagine how I felt reading those comments. I was mortified. I hated that I had autism and, at that moment, I felt like nothing worse could happen. I wanted to just crawl into a hole and disappear. When my mom found out what was happening, she pushed for disciplinary action against the bullies. However, nothing ever happened other than a quick discussion in the office with the principal. I never received a single apology—they just got away with it.

As time went on it seemed everyone else had moved on except for my family. Although the bullying had stopped, the profound effect of the words stuck with me. Whenever I made the smallest mistake or got into an argument with my family, I always heard those negative words in the back of my head. I started to believe that I was worthless and felt I should do everyone a favor and disappear. I had a plan of where and how I would end it. Thankfully a very good friend, who had gone through something similar, recognized the signs and told my mom right away. At this point, I was then taken to the hospital where I talked to lots of doctors who recommended an inpatient facility specifically for people with autism. The following day, as a bed at the facility became available, I was transferred. I had only ever been away from home for a week-long camp, but that was with my best friends—people I knew and loved. This facility was supposed to be a safe place for me to learn emotional regulation and coping skills, along with people like me.

During this experience, however, I found that these individuals had more complex challenges than I did. These individuals were experiencing behavioral challenges both in schools and at home, while my main concern was my mental health. Like most psychiatric centers, it did more harm than good. My family, however, had hoped that it would help me. After all, it was a facility for people with autism like me, so it should help, right? Wrong. Although it sounded good on paper, this was not the case. I never knew whom to trust or whether I could trust anyone at all. It was loud and scary. People were always yelling or engaging in self-injurious behaviors. I can recall moments when I was minding my own business, just showering, and would suddenly hear yelling and banging. It would make me wonder, *What did I do this time? Was I in trouble or was one of my friends in trouble*? Another memory that stands out in my mind was when I witnessed my friend being disrespectful: when this happened, I was forcing myself to try and fall asleep while other patients were yelling, and that was when I saw my friend get into a physical fight with one of the staff members. Following that incident, I remember avoiding my friend, because of the amount of anxiety and fear it actually caused me. I was so scared that if I said or did something wrong, they might yell and throw things at me like they did the staff member. Instead of reassuring us, the staff not only wanted us to continue as if nothing had happened, but they also did not advise us to leave the room for our own safety, as one would have expected.

Missed opportunities

You are probably wondering why I would tell you all of this. The answer is simple. Because we need things to change! This hospital was supposed to be one of the good ones and, even though it was allegedly one of the better facilities, it still was not equipped to help people with autism who don't fit the box. This facility was for people who had "classic" autism such as challenging behaviors as well as communication and socialization issues, not people like me who were diagnosed late and whose problems were more related to mental health. Although these specialized hospitals are supposed to be individualized, they simply are not. Despite each of us having our own goals, the way they went about treating our symptoms was not at all individualized. The hospital was very structured, which can be good for people with autism and who often do well with routines and predictability. However, it lacked the individual attention that people also needed. Instead, every patient had the same routine, group therapy, individual and family therapy, free time, and visiting hours.

This hospital had the opportunity to individualize care, especially regarding the course of treatment and types of therapies and options they allowed for patients. Psychiatric hospitals all across the world are failing people with more than one condition(Louise Whittle *et al.*, 2018). The general psychiatric centers are not equipped to treat anyone with disabilities or more complex mental health conditions besides depression and anxiety, and even then the treatment is mediocre. The specialized treatment for people with complex mental health conditions or certain disabilities is made for the "typical" look of somebody with that condition, but at the end of the day, there is no one-size-fits-all for disabilities. When you don't have that specific look, you are pushed to the side, not given adequate treatment, and discharged early because the staff would think "Oh, they seem fine." Ultimately, people with challenges that were less visible were still struggling and sent home too early. We as a country must do better for people who don't fit into these boxes. We as a nation are in a mental health crisis—we are in need of better access to mental health care. It must be made mandatory for staff to receive specific training in order to help those with more than one condition and any person with a disability (Maestri-Banks, 2019). Most treatment centers have mental health support staff; however, most of the time the positions are entry-level and the training they have had is minimal, which leads to patients not receiving adequate care.

Now you may be asking yourself, "Well you had to have gotten **something** good out of this experience right?" Unfortunately, no! What I did get out of this experience was trauma, and I, unfortunately, learned how to self-harm. I left this place in a worse headspace than I went in with, which is sadly a common occurrence for patients who enter inpatient treatment centers. A question I commonly ask myself is why? And how? Why is it that, despite our efforts to do all the right things and seek the help we need, we are still let down by the system and not receiving quality care?? And how do the administration and people higher up continuously profit off of patients when many do not truly get help? Enough is enough! We need to expose these issues and spread awareness about these problems across the country.

Returning to school

Thinking about my return to school, I didn't want or expect anything big to happen, considering I just had a school year from hell. On top of returning to school fresh out of treatment, I had to start preparing for high school. I had been in school only for a few days and my teachers were already pushing me to choose classes when I had no idea what electives and what level of classes I wanted to take. After choosing classes, teachers asked me what I wanted to do when I grew up. That day I said, "I want to do something with people with Down Syndrome." Just a few days prior, I had met a little girl with Down Syndrome at lunch and got to form a relationship with her, walk her to class, and help her at lunch. That was the day I realized that helping people with Down Syndrome was my true calling. Before that, I had several interactions with a long-time friend who has Down

Syndrome. However, I always thought I just liked her because she was sweet. I never thought I'd want to work with people with Down Syndrome. Spoiler alert—turns out this was the start of my calling and passion.

When middle school was ending, I had to go to my first Individualized Educational Planning (IEP) meeting. This was the start of something I never thought I would have to experience. All I remember during that meeting was already being so stressed because it was my first meeting. On top of that, I had to meet my new special education teacher and guidance counselor at that meeting to discuss the transition to high school and select classes.

The team argued with me that I needed the social communication class offered for students with autism. I repeatedly told the team that I did not want that, only for the guidance counselor to respond with, "Okay, well, we'll come back to that and figure it out by the start of the school year." I wish that back then I had the voice that I have today! At the time, I just sat back and nodded, thinking that **I** was the problem. Today I would have stood up for myself. She saw a young girl who was recently diagnosed with autism and had just come out of the hospital; yet she, as a seasoned guidance counselor, had biased opinions about what I could and could not do before getting to know me, simply based on my diagnosis. People just don't realize the power their words can truly have on a person. Things just got worse from there, but simply from that meeting, I felt annoyed that my opinion and voice were dismissed.

The power of words

I was yet again let down by the education system. Never in a million years would I expect a high school guidance counselor to constantly tear me down and think less of me, simply because of a diagnosis. To her, it may have been just words, but to me, it had a much deeper meaning. She told me everything I could not do at least twice a year, and those words followed me **everywhere**. Every time I made a mistake or got below a B, it all would go back to what my past bullies said to me and, now, the words of my guidance counselor. Every single time I made a mistake, I would get so mad at myself because in my mind I was proving to everyone that they were right about me and I'd just fail and struggle through high school. A guidance counselor is supposed to provide guidance and help the student feel supported and safe. My guidance counselor did the opposite and had such a profound impact on me that I still remember everything. Words **do** matter no matter the age, ability, or label.

More missed opportunities

When I first started high school, I liked my guidance counselor. I was excited to meet her and wanted to create a meaningful relationship with her. It only took about a month and a half before my guidance counselor showed her true colors and views. I don't exactly know what prompted the change in schedules, but all I remember is going from a schedule I enjoyed with fun electives to all of a sudden being put in a social communication class as well as an instructional support class. I was livid! I wondered if my team even considered what I wanted and if my voice meant anything to them.

That year, things got progressively worse. My team thought I struggled "too much" socially, and so wanted to provide additional support in that area. I was pissed. I remember sitting on a couch and talking about school during one of my therapy appointments one day when my mother mentioned something that upset me even further. She told my therapist how my team believed I struggled so much socially and that they wanted me to have a one-on-one aide to be with me during the school day. I was furious. I remember physically feeling hot from the anger, and my heart began to race. Thankfully the team did not go through with this plan. I never understood why they felt this was necessary, and I probably never will. I was not disruptive during class at all nor did I have any behavioral issues. Yes, I was socially awkward and a little hyper at times; but for the most part, I was quiet and did my work. If this required an aide for support, then half the world probably needs this as well. Sure, I experienced anxiety, but according to the National Institute for Mental Health, so do 31.1 per cent of the population in the US at some point in their lives (NIMH, 2024). I still, to this very day, do not understand why they felt I needed this. Did they ever consider the harm this could cause me? As someone already self-conscious and embarrassed, how could they possibly believe that would be helpful? Within special education, we talk a lot about fitting in and the harm labels can cause a student, so how could they not consider this? I felt that I already stuck out since the age of seven for simple things like getting pulled out of the classroom for OT or speech therapy, and here my team suggested a one-on-one aide in high school to follow me along throughout the school day. I question if they actually wanted me to stick out because I can't think of a more obvious way to stick out. And to think that wasn't the worst thing in my high school career.

The impact one bad experience can have on you

I have been through MANY IEP meetings since I was in eighth grade and I remember just how I felt in each one. But nothing will ever compare to how I felt and reacted after my sophomore year meeting, which was by far the worst one of my career and the most emotional as well. It affected me so much that, even many years later, I can still visualize the exact room and the seat I was in. I can recall how I felt, who was there, what was said, and the physical feeling I got holding back my tears. We always hear from many professionals that junior year classes are the most important for college. Therefore, this was the focus of my sophomore year IEP meeting. I chose my classes and told the team that I wanted to go to college to be a teacher. At the time, I believed they supported me. However, I found out later on that my guidance counselor thought this was not a realistic career choice for me because college would be "too hard" for me. When I found out that was how she felt, I was appalled. Like please tell me she did not just tell me, yet again, what I could not do, basically calling me "dumb" without coming out and saying it. Who would think that and, still in good conscience, believe that is okay to say that about someone? I am human and have feelings just like anybody else.

For this meeting, I had to come to school early. I recall sitting down and seeing my special education teacher who I adored, and then next to her was my guidance counselor who I did not

The system failed me, but I did not personally fail   179

like at all. I remember them asking me about my future. I said I wanted to become a life skills teacher and go to Millersville College to get my teaching degree. I also said I wanted to do an internship senior year with the life skills class. The team tried to convince me to perhaps look at jobs outside of life skills and broaden my age group. I initially thought I wanted to do only high school life skills. At the time I did not like the idea of broadening my age group as I did not like kids of any age! However, things changed a few years later, and when I told the team, my guidance counselor said, "Millersville is a four-year college and you will struggle to get into a four-year university out of high school because it requires the SATs and you will likely not get the required score." I did not like what I heard but kept it short and simple and said that I wanted to go to college no matter what. She then moved on, saying, "Well if that's the goal then we should probably get you taking harder college prep classes. But I'll be honest—I don't think you will pass." Yep, you heard me right. She said all of that and more, directly to my face.

I remember sitting there, hearing that, and feeling a terrible lump in my throat. I could feel tears filling up my eyes, but told myself I could not let them win or see me cry. So I held back the tears. Later as I was dismissed from the meeting, I left the office crying. I went to the bathroom and sobbed for a solid fifteen minutes because I was told I would never achieve my goal in life. Both my heart and my dreams were shattered. From that point on, I absolutely hated those meetings. I would feel instant stomach pains right before them due to the anxiety—the guidance counselor would be there, only to tear me down yet again. I even begged my teacher not to invite her to the meetings, but unfortunately, her attendance was a requirement.

The beginning of change

Junior year was a pretty good one, as I finally had a teacher who believed in me. My eleventh-grade history and English teacher always expressed their confidence in my ability and was always there for me—they were the bright light I needed. They were always so helpful, supportive, and, overall, just a loving human being.

In March, things took a turn when COVID-19 happened and classes got moved to Zoom. We were told grades for the fourth quarter did not matter, but I started to worry about senior year, college, and my internship, terrified that any of those are not happening anymore. One day in July, I was driving with my mom when we received a call. It was from the person in charge of the internship who informed us that the internships in elementary and middle schools were canceled. My heart sank, and I immediately started crying. I told my mom that the internship was the only good thing I had going for me and now that it was canceled, I probably wouldn't get into college. One of my biggest fears was that my guidance counselor would be proven right. I was devastated by the news, which made me sick to my stomach. During my senior year that fall, when college applications opened, I was terrified and quite literally felt like I was dying from anxiety. However, I then applied to my college, and thankfully I got in and proved everyone wrong! I thought I would finally get my happy ending and all my pain was worth it.

Later on, I graduated and went off to college. I was so excited to go to college and finally take classes to be a teacher. I thought this would be the happiest moment of my life. However, I quickly realized this was not the college for me. It was super tiny, and I was home every weekend. My friends were constantly changing, and I felt sad and out of control in both my personal and academic life. During this time, I was considering transferring to Penn State and talked it over with my parents and friends. Most were encouraging, but I had one friend tell me that I should look at schools other than Penn State's main campus, because although her boyfriend took all AP classes and got over 1210 on the SATs, he did not get in. She believed that because I did not take super hard classes and get good scores on standardized tests, I was not likely to get in. When she said all of this, my heart was crushed. I thought she was one of my best friends and was supportive of me but turns out that was not the case. I was sad but I continued to believe it was an honest mistake and that she cared about me. In spite of her discouragement, I still applied. I waited a month before I got an email one night that I had been accepted into the College of Education at Penn State University (PSU) Park! I was so beyond excited. Then, later that week, I committed to Penn State and started at the PSU the following semester.

The challenge of change

Although I was beyond happy at Penn State, I also felt a lack of support from friends. That change was hard for me. To cope with this and my emotions, I developed an unhealthy coping mechanism and eventually became anorexic. During this time, I was dropping weight very quickly and acting on unhealthy behaviors. Naturally, I hid this fact from my family but bragged about it to my friends. My friends were concerned and tried to push me to seek help. I did not think I had an issue, so I resisted help. These friends I had for years suddenly stopped supporting me and being my friend. Things quickly got worse and physically it all started to take a toll on me.

In May, I went to a specialist, and the doctor recommended a higher level of care such as an inpatient or residential program. I started flipping out because I was worried about how I was going to handle this along with work. I did not want any of them to know. In June, I came to terms with the fact that I needed this additional support, so I went to a specialized eating disorders inpatient facility. I was at the facility for about five and a half weeks. This was by far one of the worst experiences of my life.

When "help" is actually harm: take two

I went from having all my independence to going into treatment where I was stripped of independence. We had to shower only in the morning, get up at like 5 am for vitals, get poked with needles once a week, and get blood sugar checked at 3 am every single day for the first week of treatment. We also could use the bathroom only at certain times of the day. If we requested an emergency bathroom use, we had to keep the door wide open while the staff was in there because of the risk of purging. This was protocol, even if that was not one of your behaviors. Overall, there were so many rules that were not healthy for anyone with

The system failed me, but I did not personally fail   183

an eating disorder, let alone those who also have autism. If you had even one noodle left on your plate, the staff marked it incomplete, and you would have to drink a can of Ensure or two. You had 45 minutes to finish your meals; if you did not, you had an extra item added to the next meal. Having only that much time to finish a meal was ridiculous for an eating disorder unit. We also had a limit on the amount of water we could have and when. We could only have one cup of water thrice a day and at meals, but if you were still thirsty after the meal or did not finish it, the staff could refuse you water, since sometimes people use it to fill up and control hunger cues. The overall setting was just horrible no matter what. It was extremely stressful and loud. There was always someone screaming, phones ringing, and codes going off on the overhead speaker. We were not allowed to flush the toilets as staff had to check. This environment was not healthy or set up for quality treatment let alone those with disabilities. For people with anxiety or disabilities, it was extremely loud and overwhelming, eventually setting us up to fail.

I was discharged after five and a half weeks because I finished one meal. The rule was, that if you were able to finish ONE meal you could be discharged. Don't get me wrong—I was excited to have my freedom again. However, do I think it was the appropriate time? No. I went to an outpatient PHP program and kept up with meals for a solid three days before quitting and relapsing.

Just like many specialized centers, the policies, environment, and procedures were not set up to help patients succeed. Any person would be on edge and snippy if they were being rushed to eat and sleep deprived, let alone a person with a mental illness or other types of disabilities. This hospital was not set up to be inclusive of people who have different experiences such as autism or other disabilities or even somebody with nontraditional eating disorders that are less restrictive. As a country, we need to do better at creating healthier environments at psychiatric facilities. The ambiance should be calming and safe, not loud and scary. People should not be having multiple panic attacks a day. The sensory environment should not be so overwhelming that the patient ends up having some type of behavioral episode. Patients should feel safe, loved, and respected; instead, we all felt terrified, especially those who were part of the LGBTQ+ community. The number of times I witnessed staff mistreat, deadname, or use wrong pronouns is NOT OKAY! Deadnaming refers to the improper use of a transgender or nonbinary person's birth or legal name after they have chosen a new name that better aligns with their identity (Cleveland Clinic, 2021). This can be harmful because it can lead to a person experiencing more anxiety and depression. These were my friends, and I saw the impact that an unhealthy environment had on them. We need more training and stricter requirements for staff working at these centers and, most importantly, better environments and policies for working with diverse populations, especially those who have identities that are multiply marginalized and who experience intersectionality. How are we supposed to heal if the environment itself is terrifying and causes more trauma? I can say without a doubt that I came out of this place with nothing good besides friends. I honestly came out worse, feeling invalidated in my struggles with the addiction, and burdened with even more trauma. This needs to change! The future generation deserves better. They are entitled to receive quality care in a safe and calm environment.

The system *must* change

You may be thinking, **Wow you have been through a ton of things**. Yes, I have, and no, I did not deserve any of it. However, it did help me appreciate more things in life that many people overlook and take for granted. You may also be feeling bad for me or giving me sympathy, like **Awe, poor Jenna has autism and all these mental health challenges.** Well, don't feel bad! I worked through these challenges and now am the happiest I've ever been. I've met some of the best people ever through these journeys. I have also encountered some not-so-amazing people, but I have learned how to deal with this also.

You may wonder why would I write all of this and be so vulnerable. I wrote it for two big reasons. First, there are others out there who are struggling with similar challenges. I want them to know that they are never alone and things improve with hard work. I want them to know that anything is possible, especially happiness.

Second, I also wrote this chapter for people to evaluate themselves on their perspectives on people with disabilities. People with disabilities are just like anybody else and have feelings and challenges just like anyone else. They deserve positive people and support in their lives too. It is simply not okay to think less of the disability community simply because of a diagnosis. People with disabilities are successful just like anyone else. Even when you can't see all disabilities, the challenges they experience are still valid. People everywhere see disability as a terrible thing, and this way of thinking is simply not okay. Having ableist views is not okay! If you see or hear something ableist, it is our job as part of society to stand up and call people out on their views. We can't expect change if we sit back and say nothing, without educating society. It's time to change the system!

Dear friends in the struggle

To anyone struggling out there, know that I support you and always will. You can and will prove people wrong. You will find people who love you for who you are. Just like anyone else, you deserve happiness and joy. I know life is hard with the failed system we live in. It is a place where ableism is so normalized and considered okay—but know it's not. Your feelings are valid, and you can and should stand up for yourself. I promise you that when you do, you are not being mean. You are educating people and being a part of a community standing up for each other. If we stay silent, the system may never change. I speak up and stand up for myself and others because the future generation deserves to know that they are worthy of love and happiness and that it does get better. I never thought it would be for me either, but here I am, a junior at Penn State, majoring in special education, and on the road to becoming a teacher. I have met the most amazing people along the way. I never imagined that through this major, and the clubs I am a part of, I would find my best friends. I've known some people for only five months and I already adore them. This is possible for you too!

Friends, family, and special shoutouts

Family:

To my family, who walked beside me throughout this journey, thank you! Although at times it has not been easy for any of us, I am incredibly grateful to have grown up in a caring, loving, and understanding family that continues to try to learn about the flaws of the education system. I would not be who I am today without you all pushing me to be my best while also loving and supporting me. From the bottom of my heart, thank you for walking with me on this journey.

Friends:

To all my amazing friends who have stayed with me throughout this journey, thank you! I just want to express the overall gratitude I have for each of you. Whether you have been my friend for many years or you just met me recently, you have made an impact on my life and I am incredibly grateful to call you all my friends. You all give me hope and show me what true friends are, and I will forever be grateful for that. I know at times friendship has been complicated with me, but I just want to say I love you all and am so grateful and lucky to have such amazing friends who are so patient, understanding, accepting, and always willing to do anything for me. Not everyone gets friends like you, so I consider myself lucky and will never stop telling the world how amazing each of you are. From the bottom of my heart, thank you for being my friend!

Camp Kesem Central, PA:

To all the amazing members, thank you. From the first meeting, I have felt at home with Kesem simply because each member has gone out of their way for me by making an effort to get to know me. Kesem came into my life after a rather dark period, and I was met with nothing but love and acceptance. I will forever be grateful for that. After losing a community I thought was forever, you can imagine how hard it was to jump into a new organization. Boy, am I glad that I did! I can confidently say that if I had seven hours left, I would want to spend it with all of you. I feel so lucky and honored to have met you all and call you my best friends! You all came into my life much later than most of my friends, but I wouldn't change a thing about it. You all showed me what true friends are and helped me trust people again. After sharing my story, all I remember is how much love, acceptance, and understanding I was met with and I will always be grateful for that. Thank you all for being you and loving me unconditionally. I love you all and thank you for everything.

My Best Friend:

To my Kesem BIG homefries, thank you! Thank you for being the absolute best BIG and best friend I could have ever possibly wished for. From Kesem BIG to best friends, I am so happy it turned out this way. You have helped me so much in the past year, and I will always be in awe of the love you have shown me. You have truly shown me how to trust people again and what a true friend looks like. I remember since losing my ex-best friend I thought I was not lovable and deserving of a best friend that loves me as much as I love them. You showed me a little after a March during a event this could not be further from the truth. I remember I told you for the first time that you were my best friend after I narrated my story, and you basically said I was yours too. I will truly appreciate that for the rest of my life as when you said it I cried tears of joy because never have I ever experienced a best friend of mine tell me that I was also their best friend. I will forever be grateful for this friendship we've created! Even after finding out basically everything I've been through, you still continued to show up for me and show me through actions not words that you care about me and that I am your best friend! You constantly let me talk about the same things over and over again, listen to me and my feelings, and put up with my at-times chaotic and overly attached personality. Despite all of that, you still accept me and love me for who I am and have done so much for me, including giving me rides home and bringing me snacks when I have long days of class and training. I will always be grateful to have you in my life and to be known as starbies. Thank you for being you and showing me what a true friend is and letting me know that it's okay to trust people and myself again. You've shown me nothing but love, joy, and acceptance, and that you are here to stay forever no matter what. Given what my past best friend did, it means the world to me that you continue to show up for me, call me out, and keep me safe when needed. Although nobody enjoys being called out or parented by their friends, it shows me just how much you care about me and that you're a true friend who's here to stay. It means the absolute world to me that you care about me this deeply. I will always cherish our friendship, and our friendship will always be my favorite! Thank you for being the absolute best thing to happen to me this past year! I will continue to brag about what a great friend I have and how proud of him I am! Thank you for being such an amazing friend and always accepting me as a human being without judgment!

Special thanks:

To the special people who have impacted my life in a positive way, thank you! I am grateful to the teachers and professionals who were always so kind, understanding, and accepting of me and all I've been through! Mrs Radel, Miss Goodman, and the entire history wing, especially Mrs Bartal and Mr Fackler, thank you! Thank you for always believing in me and showing me I can do hard things and for filling my days with lots of joy and laughter when I needed it most! When I felt so alone and felt nobody believed I could do it, you guys did and I will forever be grateful for that! To Ms Hiler, thank you for getting me to this point and being one of the good and trustworthy professionals! You have no idea how rare that is and I truly appreciated you back then and to this day. I am where I am today because of you, and I will never forget you and will never be able to express my gratitude to you! Thank you for everything! To Maggie Kutz, Nina Pace, Ryan Poster, and their families, thank you! Thank you for being my why and for teaching me so much about special education! Most importantly, thank you for giving me so much love as well as for instilling love and passion for this field in me in addition to helping me realize I want to make real change in this field!

Xoxo,

Jenna

Reflective questions

1. How does this story illustrate the ways in which the systems fail to understand and provide care for people with autism who also have mental health support needs? How can these systems do harm instead of providing quality care?

2. Why is it important for school counselors to not be ableist? How can they serve as gatekeepers to opportunities?

3. Even though the educational and healthcare systems failed the author, how is she advocating for herself? What qualities does she have that will make her a critical supporter for her future students in special education?

4. What are some ways you can ensure that girls with autism are also supported in their mental, emotional, and physical health? How can you help them to feel empowered to pursue their dreams and goals?

5. Despite the challenges of feeling alone and unworthy of love, what are ways the author has felt loved throughout the journey?

Notes

1. Learning Disability is one of the 13 federally recognized disabilities, see https://sites.ed.gov/idea/regs/b/a/300.8/c/10

2. See American Academy of Audiology, "Auditory Processing Disorder" found at https://www.audiology.org/consumers-and-patients/hearing-and-balance/auditory-processing-disorders/

3. The Individuals with Disabilities Education Act, also known as IDEA, reauthorized in 2004, is part of US special education law that guarantees a "free and appropriate public education" for students with disabilities.

4. Hershey Medical Center is a hospital located in the state of Pennsylvania.

5. Individualized Family Services Plans are covered under Part C of the Individuals with Disabilities Education Act (IDEA, 2004) and serve children from birth to three years of age.

6. Individualized Educational Plans are covered under Part B of the Individuals with Disabilities Education Act (IDEA, 2004) and serve children from age 3 to 21 years of age, or whenever the student transitions from secondary school.

7. Gifted Individualized Educational Plan

8. Vocational technical center

9. Rensselaer Polytechnic Institute

10. Family Education Rights and Privacy Act

11. Paw Patrol is a children's cartoon show that features rescue dogs who offer their help in response to neighborhood emergencies.

12. Immigration and Customs Enforcement (ICE), a US agency that regulates cross-border immigration. Many people have been detained under ICE enforcement, subjected to the policies enforced under different administrations.

13. Although this word has been used in history, recognizing the harmful and stigmatizing nature of this word, Rosa's Law was passed in the United States 2010 to change this to intellectual disability. In addition, many organizations in the US have promoted campaigns, such as "End the R-Word", as a movement to stop the use of this term in everyday language.

14. Tertiary level refers to college and university level educational levels.

15. Although this is now known to fall under the category of Autism Spectrum Disorder (ASD), Asperger's Syndrome was once perceived as a separate diagnostic category.

16. The Autism Diagnostic Observation Schedule (ADOS) is a standardized diagnostic evaluation to assess whether a child has autism based on direct observations of their behavior, as well as the child's developmental age and levels (Akshoomoff *et al.*, 2006).

17. Praxis® Examinations (provided through the Educational Testing Service (ETS) examine teacher candidates' core, subject, and content area knowledge, in preparation for educator certification.

18. Rosa's Law was administered in 2010 under the Obama administration in order to change from the stigmatizing label of "mental retardation" to "intellectual disability" on most legal documentation.

References

Akshoomoff, N., Corsello, C. and Schmidt, H. (2006). The Role of the Autism Diagnostic Observation Schedule in the Assessment of Autism Spectrum Disorders in School and Community Settings. *The California School Psychologist*, 11(1), pp. 7–19.

Alur, M. (2021). Disabled in India… A Charity Model? *Journal of Medical Evidence*, 2(1), pp. 50–58.

American Academy of Audiology. Auditory Processing Disorder. [Online] Available at: www.audiology.org/consumers-and-patients/hearing-and-balance/auditory-processing-disorders/. Accessed March 9, 2024.

Austermann, Q., Gelbar, N., Reis, S. and Madaus, J. (2023). The Transition to College: Lived Experiences of Academically Talented Students with Autism. *Frontiers in Psychiatry*, 14, p. 1125904.

Bakthavachalu, P., Kannan, S. M. and Qoronfleh, M. W. (2020). Food Color and Autism: A Meta-Analysis. *Advances in Neurobiology*, 24, pp. 481–504.

Bal, A., Betters-Bubon, J. and Fish, R. E. (2019). A Multilevel Analysis of Statewide Disproportionality in Exclusionary Discipline and the Identification of Emotional Disturbance. *Education and Urban Society*, 51(2), pp. 247–268.

Bayes, D. A., Heath, A. K., Williams, C., & Ganz, J. B. (2013). Pardon the interruption: Enhancing communication skills for students with intellectual disability. *Teaching exceptional children*, *45*(3), pp. 64–70.

Boyce, S. (2020). *Disparities Within School Discipline: An Examination of Race, English Language Learner Status, & Suspension*. Mankato, MN: Minnesota State University.

Brewer, R. and Murphy, J. (2016, July 14). People with Autism Can Read Emotions, Feel Empathy. *Scientific American*. Available at: www.scientificamerican.com/article/people-with-autism-can-read-emotions-feel-empathy1/. Accessed March 9, 2024.

Clinic, T. C. (2021). Why deadnaming is harmful. [Online] Available at: https://health.clevelandclinic.org/deadnaming Accessed February 26, 2024.

Connor, D. J., and Ferri, B. A. (2005). Integration and Inclusion—A Troubling Nexus: Race, Disability, and Special Education. *The Journal of African American History*, 90(1–2), pp. 107–127.

Connor, E. O., & Corcoran, Y. (2022). Caring for a child with a life limiting condition: The experiences of nurses in an intellectual disability service provider. *Journal of Intellectual Disabilities*, *26*(4), pp. 938–953.

Dunn, D. (2021, December 15). understanding ableism and negative reactions to disability. [Online] American Psychological Association. Available at: www.apa.org/ed/precollege/psychology-teacher-network/introductory-psychology/ableism-negative-reactions-disability. Accessed February 26, 2024.

Ewing, J. (2024, January 24). How to use chunking in the classroom. [Online] Edutopia; George Lucas Educational Foundation. Available at: www.edutopia.org/article/chunking-content-classroom/. Accessed March 2, 2024.

Flores Martin, A. C. (2022). *A qualitative study: parental involvement as defined by parents and special educators*. Doctoral dissertation. Rutgers University-Graduate School of Education.

García, O., Kleifgen, J. A. and Falchi, L. (2008). From English Language Learners to Emergent Bilinguals. *Equity Matters*. Research Review No. 1. Campaign for Educational Equity, Teachers College, Columbia University.

Gorski, P. C. and Pothini, S. G. (2013). *Case Studies on Diversity and Social Justice Education*. London: Routledge.

Hamayan, E., Marler, B., Sánchez-López, C., Alfredo, A., & Damico, J. (2023). *Special education considerations for multilingual learners: Delivering a continuum of services*. Brookes Publishing Company. PO Box 10624, Baltimore, MD 21285.

hooks, bell. (1994). *Teaching to Transgress: Education as the Practice of Freedom*. London: Routledge.

Hume R. and Burgess, H. (2021, September 1). "I'm Human After All": Autism, Trauma, and Affective Empathy. *Autism Adulthood*, 3(3), pp. 221–229. DOI: 10.1089/aut.2020.0013.

Individuals with Disabilities Education Act (IDEA) (2004) Learning Disabilities. *Sec. 300.8 (C) (10)* (2018). *Individuals with Disabilities Education Act*. Available at: https://sites.ed.gov/idea/regs/b/a/300.8/c/10

Kida, T. E. (2006). *Don't believe everything you think: the 6 basic mistakes we make in thinking*. Prometheus Books.

Khan, S. (2021). Cultural humility vs. cultural competence—and why providers need both. [Online] Health City. Available at: https://healthcity.bmc.org/policy-and-industry/cultural-humility-vs-cultural-competence-providers-need-both. Accessed February 19, 2024.

Lalvani, P. and Hale, C. (2015). Squeaky Wheels, Mothers from Hell, and CEOs of the IEP: Parents, Privilege, and the "Fight" for Inclusive Education. *Understanding and Dismantling Privilege*, 5(2), pp. 21–41.

Maestri-Banks, A. (2019). One Size Does Not Fit All: Mental Health Services Access for People with Intellectual/Learning Disability Requires Individualised Planning and Education/Training Programmes for Health and Social Care Providers. *Evidence-Based Nursing*, 23(4), p. 107.

Malapela, R. G., & Thupayagale-Tshweneagae, G. (2024). Enablers to enhance school-based adolescents with intellectual disabilities' learning: A narrative approach. *Journal of Intellectual Disabilities*, *28*(1), 83–92.

Manago, B., Davis, J. L. and Goar, C. (2017). Discourse in Action: Parents' Use of Medical and Social Models to Resist Disability Stigma. *Social Science & Medicine*, 184, pp. 169–177.

Miller, D., Rees, J. and Pearson, A. (2021). "Masking Is life": Experiences of Masking in Autistic and Nonautistic adults. *Autism in Adulthood*, 3(4), pp. 330–338.

Pulrang, A. (2023, January 13). *It's Time to Stop Even Casually Misusing Disability Words*. [Online] Forbes. Available at: www.for bes.com/sites/andrewpulrang/2021/02/20/its-time-to-stop-even-casually-misusing-disability-words/?sh=779334907d4e. Accessed February 19, 2024.

Quinn, M. E., Hunter, C. L., Ray, S., Rimon, M. M. Q., Sen, K. and Cumming, R. (2016). The Double Burden: Barriers and Facilitators to Socioeconomic Inclusion for Women with Disability in Bangladesh. *Disability, CBR & Inclusive Development*, 27(2), pp. 128–149.

Rao, S. (2024). A Journey across Countries, Constructs, and Dreams: Perspectives of Indian American Families of Youth with Developmental Disabilities on Transition from School to Post-School Settings. *American Journal of Qualitative Research*, 8(1), pp. 133–156.

Roy, N., Amin, M. B., Mamun, M. A., Sarker, B., Hossain, E. and Aktarujjaman, M. (2023). Prevalence and Factors Associated with Depression, Anxiety, and Stress among People with Disabilities during COVID-19 Pandemic in Bangladesh: A Cross-Sectional Study. *PLOS ONE*, 18(7), 1–14. DOI:10.1371/journal.pone.0288322

Safta-Zecheria, L. (2018). The Infantilization of Intellectual Disability and Political Inclusion: A Pedagogical Approach. *Journal of Educational Sciences*, 19, pp. 104–112.

Shohel, T.A., Nasrin, N., Farjana, F., Shovo, T., Asha, A. R., Heme, M. A., Islam, A., Paul, P. and Hossain, M. H. (2022). *"He Was a Brilliant Student but Became Mad Like His Grandfather"*: An Exploratory Investigation on the Social Perception and Stigma Against Individuals Living with Mental Health Problems in Bangladesh. *BMC Psychiatry*, 22(702), 1–11. DOI: 10.1186/s12888-022-04359-3

Tatum, B. D. (1997). *Why Are All the Black Kids Sitting Together in the Cafeteria. And Other Conversations About Race.* New York: Basic Books.

Yosso, T. J. (2005). Whose Culture Has Capital? A Critical Race Theory Discussion of Community Cultural Wealth. *Race Ethnicity and Education*, 8(1), pp. 69–91.

Zeitlin, V. and Curcic, S. (2014). Parental Voices on Individualized Education Programs: "Oh, IEP Meeting Tomorrow? Rum Tonight!", *Disability & Society*, 29(3), 373–387, DOI: 10.1080/09687599.2013.776493

Notes on Contributors

Editors

Lydia Ocasio-Stoutenburg is Assistant Professor of Special Education at the Pennsylvania State University. Her scholarship, teaching, and service focus on equity, responding to the unceasing need to advocate for systems to better support people with multiple marginalized social identities as well as their families. As a critical and intersectional qualitative inquirer, Lydia's research focuses on amplifying the voices of individuals and families who have been historically marginalized in research and by policy and practice.

Yuchen Yang is a PhD candidate in Curriculum and Instruction at the Pennsylvania State University, specializing in early childhood education. His research and career interests are centered on exploring and understanding the nuanced dynamics of teacher-parent relationships in early childhood education settings, particularly from a social class perspective. He is also dedicated to promoting participatory actions that aim to fulfill parents' needs, enhance teachers' well-being, and foster positive interactions between teachers and parents.

Contributors

Karla Patricia Armendariz is a Mexican cisgender female who is currently a doctoral candidate and a bilingual speech-language pathologist. Karla's deep commitment to her work is reflected in her hands-on experience with the culturally linguistically diverse disability community. She has served as a paraprofessional, worked with a theater company for exceptional students, and held the post of a program director for a nonprofit serving adults on the spectrum.

Azaria Cunningham received her PhD in Curriculum and Instruction at the Pennsylvania State University. Azaria earned her bachelor's, master's, and Supervisory Certification at the William Paterson University, New Jersey. She has completed her bachelor's in integrated mathematics and science with a double major in K-6 elementary and (6-8) middle school science education specialization. Azaria worked as a science teacher in the K-12 public school system for six years. Her research interest resides in understanding how pre-service and teacher educators learn within university-based and school-based contexts through teacher-driven mechanisms such as real-time coaching, mentoring, and supervision practices.

Aimee Granada-Jeronimo graduated from the Pennsylvania State University with a bachelor's degree in special education. Inspired by her own learning disability, she is determined to fulfill her lifelong dream of teaching and advocating for students with disabilities. With continued support from her parents and twin sister, Aimee is excited to begin her teaching journey. She is forever grateful for all the knowledge and experiences she has gained and cannot wait to continue to learn and grow as an educator.

Ava Herr is a fourth year student at the Pennsylvania State University with a focus on achieving a bachelor's degree in special education by 2025. After graduation, Ava hopes to continue their education while working with "the littles" at an IU8 or HeadStart facility while continuing to help students through the Gwen's Girls organization. In particular, Ava hopes to work with young girls on the autism spectrum to assist their families in the early intervention process while also furthering research on diagnosing women on the spectrum. Ava is currently working multiple jobs to make a difference in the disability community.

Ruby Humphris graduated from Penn State University's Special Education program with a master's degree in special education and has started her doctoral study in special education at Penn State. Her research interests range from examining how best to make augmentative and alternative communication (AAC) accessible, representative, and code-switching friendly for multilingual students and their families, examining the need for true collaboration between all members of a student's Individualized Education Plan (IEP) team, using an intersectionality perspective when engaging all members of the student's support team, and most notability transition services planning and familial engagement. Ruby is a mother to nine beautiful children who are and have always been her why.

Courtney Kehoe is a graduate of Penn State University's Special Education program, receiving a bachelor's degree in special education. Courtney has wanted to teach for as long as she can remember and is looking forward to pursuing her dreams this coming year. When she is not in the classroom, she enjoys listening to music, watching Philadelphia sports with her family, and spending time with loved ones.

Nayma Sultana Mim is a PhD candidate in special education at Penn State University. She has received bachelor's and master's degrees in special education from the University of Dhaka, Bangladesh. Her research interests include exploring the experiences of marginalized students with disabilities and their families using the lens of intersectionality and teacher education.

Dana Patenaude is a PhD candidate in special education at Penn State University. She has degrees in early intervention and applied behavior analysis. Dana has worked previously as a Board Certified Behavior Analyst and is currently conducting research regarding Augmentative and Alternative Communication (AAC) interventions for children with limited speech for perception expression, and strengthening interprofessional collaborations.

Millie Rodríguez, MSEd, is a Project FUTURE Fellow and PhD candidate at Penn State University researching strategies to support twice exceptional (2e) students during their transition to college. She is also interested in 2e persistence to graduation, particularly for first-generation students and those from underrepresented groups.

Jenna Spencer is a senior majoring in special education at Penn State University. Jenna's goal is to become a special education teacher, while also continuing to serve as an advocate for students with disabilities. Jenna wants to continue to make a difference in the special education system because of what she went through as a student. She hopes to become a teacher and later influence policy changes in her field. Jenna is involved with organizations such as Penn state homecoming, Penn state THON, Central Pa Camp Kesem, working at Easter seals in State College. In addition, she has also worked at a special needs summer camp counselor for children and adults with IDD.

Bianca Emma Stoutenburg is a senior majoring in psychology with a minor in special education at the Pennsylvania State University. An avid reader, Bianca loves writing to celebrate and embrace her creativity in her spare time. She loves spending time with her family and friends, and seeks beauty and the expression of love in all areas of life.

Julia Sledz graduated with a bachelor's degree in special education from Penn State University. She is looking forward to using her degree to advocate for and support students with disabilities. In her spare time, Julia can be found reading, playing volleyball, and cheering for every Penn State sports team possible.

Rebecca Zinn is a senior studying special education at Pennsylvania State University. Her experience growing up with an older brother was different from the other older brothers she knew, alongside her parents' determination to give him his best chance, inspired Rebecca to start working with children when she was in middle school. Toward this goal, she continues to pursue teaching, learning, and advocacy for the rest of her life.

Index

AAC. *see* Augmentative and alternative communication (AAC)

Ableism. 17, 108, 165, 186

Academic. 38, 86, 106, 108, 160, 161, 162, 168, 181

Accommodations. 69, 70, 71, 138

ADA. *see* Americans with Disabilities (ADA)

ADHD. 152

Adopted. 166

ADOS. 131

Advocacy. xxii, xxiii, 24, 41, 44, 46, 73, 86, 136, 139, 142, 160, 162

Advocate. xxi, 24, 30, 46, 50, 59, 72, 86, 91, 96, 139, 141, 150, 165

Americans with Disabilities (ADA). 45

Appointments. 114

Artistic. 63, 75, 130

Auditory process disorder. 4

Augmentative and alternative communication (AAC). 51, 54, 90, 149

Autism. xxi, 9, 10, 16, 19, 21, 22, 24, 26, 29, 31, 32, 33, 34, 36, 37, 38, 39, 50, 54, 79, 80, 82, 83, 84, 89, 91, 125, 126, 127, 131, 133, 148, 168, 169, 170, 171, 172, 175, 183, 184, 185

Autism Spectrum Disorder (ASD). 30, 37, 42, 148

Behavior analytic. 60

Cerebral palsy. 91

Childhood post traumatic stress disorder (cPTSD). 131

College applications. 180

Communications. 29, 31, 32, 38, 50, 54, 59, 62, 64, 73, 80, 148, 149, 150, 160, 172, 175, 176

Compassion. 17

Concussions. 69, 70, 71

Cortical visual impairment. 155

COVID-19. 62, 180

Creative. 63

Cultural. xiv

Deficit. xxii, 96, 108, 152, 162

206 Love is Praxis

Developmental delays. 133

Diagnosed. *see* Diagnosis

Diagnosis. xxii, 5, 33, 37, 38, 51, 81, 82, 84, 126, 133, 147, 151, 155, 156, 158, 161, 166, 167, 168, 169, 170, 175, 185

Disability community. 6, 71, 111, 133, 185

Disabled. xvii, xix, xxi, 103

Discrimination. 2, 101, 147

Down Syndrome. xii, 81, 89, 91, 95, 174, 175

Education. xi, xvii, xxi, xxii, xxiii, 3, 6, 24, 25, 30, 34, 38, 44, 45, 46, 71, 72, 74, 80, 82, 84, 92, 101, 102, 103, 105, 108, 135, 137, 138, 139, 141, 142, 159, 162, 166, 167, 168, 169, 175, 176, 177, 178, 186, 187, 190

Emotional/Behavioral Disturbance (EBD). 41

Empower. 6

English language learners. 2, 137

Enrichment. 29

Epilepsy. 155

Families. xxi, 5, 26, 30, 35, 46, 49, 55, 59, 61, 62, 64, 65, 67, 73, 77, 83, 84, 85, 86, 87, 100, 103, 107, 109, 128, 143, 150, 156, 159, 160, 163

Gay. 2, 5, 36

Gifted. 29

Grandmother. 112

Guidance. 42, 64, 175, 176, 178, 179, 180

Head/brain trauma. 146

HeadStart. 114, 115, 116, 117

Heteronormative. 2

Homogeneous. 2

Hope. xx, xxii, xxiii, 26, 30, 43, 49, 66, 67, 86, 87, 159

IDEA. 160

Immigrants. 2, 4, 77, 78, 79

Individualized. 168

Individualized Education Plan (IEP). 33

Individualized Family Services Plan (IFSP). 33

Infantilizing. 92, 96

Intellectual disability (IDD). 19, 148, 155, 156, 162, 193

Intersectionality. 2, 4, 184

Joy. 3, 81, 83, 189

Kindergarten. 24, 116, 117

Label. 5, 75, 76, 96, 133, 134, 138, 161, 170, 177, 193

Language. xvii, 2, 4, 5, 33, 39, 51, 152

Learning disability. 4, 5, 108

Index   207

Love. xi, xii, xix, xx, xxi, 6, 13, 18, 20, 23, 30, 35, 43, 49, 66, 96, 103, 129, 157, 186, 189

Masking. 19

Medical services. 102

Mental health. 43, 105, 107, 167, 168, 169, 171, 173

Microcephaly. 155, 158

Milestones. 147

Myths. 99

Neurodivergence (ND). 30, 37, 133, 146

Neurotypical. 22, 25, 146

Nonbinary. 29

Opportunities. 24, 26, 30, 38, 46, 102, 105, 106, 117, 133, 140, 173

Paraprofessional. 60, 73, 74, 75, 77, 81, 86, 124, 137, 139

Pervasive Development Disorder-Not Otherwise Specified (PDD-NOS). 33

Potty training. 52, 76

Practitioners. 49

Pray. 90, 101, 169

Preeclampsia. 146

Protective. xvii, 9, 12

Rehabilitation. 102

Self-regulation. 34

Sensory. 11, 32, 34, 113, 155, 166, 184

Sibling. xx, xxii, 9, 10, 12, 21, 22, 24, 36, 50, 59

Socializing. 107

Special education. xxiii, 24, 92

Speech and language therapist. 149

Stigmas. 26, 107, 138, 140, 147

Stigmatized. *see* Stigmas

Suicidal ideation. 37, 40, 45

Superstitions. 99

Teach. 6

Tertiary level. 104

Tokenization. 78

Transformative. xx

Unmask. 19

Utilitarian. 102

Voices. xv, xxi, xxii, 4, 18, 40, 53, 54, 78, 86, 107, 136, 139, 149, 165, 175, 176

Vulnerable. 86, 102, 103, 185

Women with disabilities. 101, 102, 103, 105, 106, 108, 109

www.ingramcontent.com/pod-product-compliance
Lightning Source LLC
LaVergne TN
LVHW021129201224
799493LV00021B/1039